UML Xtra-Light

UML Xtra-Light

How to Specify Your Software Requirements

Milan Kratochvíl   **Barry McGibbon**

PUBLISHED BY THE PRESS SYNDICATE OF THE UNIVERSITY OF CAMBRIDGE
The Pitt Building, Trumpington Street, Cambridge, United Kingdom

CAMBRIDGE UNIVERSITY PRESS
The Edinburgh Building, Cambridge CB2 2RU, UK
40 West 20th Street, New York, NY 10011–4211, USA
477 Williamstown Road, Port Melbourne, VIC 3207, Australia
Ruiz de Alarcón 13, 28014 Madrid, Spain
Dock House, The Waterfront, Cape Town 8001, South Africa

http://www.cambridge.org

First published 2003

Printed in the United States of America

Typefaces Stone Serif 10.5/13 pt., Stone Sans, and Informal   *System* QuarkXPress®   [GH]

A catalogue record for this book is available from the British Library.

Library of Congress Cataloging in Publication Data

Kratochvíl, Milan.
    UML xtra-light : how to specify your software requirements / Milan Kratochvíl,
Barry McGibbon.
        p. cm.
    Includes bibliographical references and index.
    ISBN 0-521-89242-2
    1. Application software – Development. 2. UML (Computer science) I. McGibbon,
Barry, 1947– II. Title.
QA76.76.A65 K72 2002
005.1 – dc21
                                                                                  200219253
    ISBN 0 521 89242 2 paperback

To my father, Jiří, and to generations of composers
before him who realized that architectural
standards, components, and reuse
all boost creativity and invention.

Milan Kratochvíl

To my wife, Vicky, for her lifetime
of love and support

Barry McGibbon

Contents

Foreword   ix

Preface   xi

Acknowledgments   xiii

About the Authors   xv

How to Customize This Book   xvii

Chapter 1 • Introduction   1

Software – Yet Another Knowledge Industry   1
Classifying the Knowledge Industry   2
Consequences of the Knowledge Industry   3
Sharing the Knowledge   5
Sharing the Responsibility for Getting It Right   6
Methods and Processes   8
Summary   11

Chapter 2 • Aligning to the Business   13

Using UML Activity Diagrams   15
Using Business Use-Case Diagrams   23
But What About the Data?   25
Summary   26

Chapter 3 • Adding Rigor to the Requirements 27

Use Cases 27
Use-Case Example 29
Meeting the Devil 34
Use-Case Analysis at Two Levels, At Least 36
How to Avoid Messing Up Use Cases 39
Summary 46

Chapter 4 • Sketching the Inside Structure 47

Class Diagrams 48
The Class Diagram 50
Understanding Class Relationships 52
Summary 59

Chapter 5 • Sketching the Inside Dynamics 61

State Diagrams 61
Tying It All Together 67
UML Collaboration Diagrams 70
Other UML Diagrams 70
Summary 71

Chapter 6 • Moving Toward Components 73

Components Communicate with Everyone 76
Impact of the Component-Based Approach 79
Reusing Components 81
Building a Component Library 83
Sharing Components in Your Organization 84
Avoiding the Traps 85
Automating the Bid Process 87
Summary 88

Chapter 7 • Mapping from Classes to Data Models 89

Use Appropriate Diagrams and Standards 90
Mapping Relationships 91
Summary 95

Chapter 8 • Concluding Remarks 97

Think Big, Start Small, and Sustain the Effort 97
UML Under Time Constraints 98

Some Suggested Readings 101
Index 103

Foreword

Yet another book about UML! Since its initial version, the Unified Modeling Language has gone an impressive way in the IT community. Over the past couple of years, we have been loading our bookcase with quite a few UML books. Many of them deal with applying or extending UML for a specific domain: UML for project management, UML for business modeling, UML for Java, real-time UML, UML for components, UML for web applications, and so forth.

This book takes a somewhat different and, in our opinion, long-awaited approach. It goes back to the *basics* of UML: *improving the communication* among different stakeholders of a (software) project. As the authors of the book write: "a UML made easy for people who specify, buy, or manage complex software systems." Many of these stakeholders are non-IT professionals in much need of an easy-to-digest introduction to UML.

Looking back on the IBM SanFrancisco project – one of the *real success projects* in the field of object-oriented *business applications* – where we, at IBS, played a central role as initiators and principal development partner to IBM, a key success factor was the alignment among domain experts, sponsors, and object experts – through a minimum set of concepts and techniques.

In addition, this book focuses on the new paradigm in software development: fast delivery of applications based on components sourced from various suppliers. Even though UML initially placed considerable focus on creating applications from scratch, successful software projects today are all about *creating, buying, and integrating software components.* This leaves us (who intend to stay competitive and successful!) extremely dependent on a *standard notation* for any software-related communication, specification, and knowledge sharing. The IBM SanFrancisco/WebSphere Business components provide an extreme case for this. By using a standard notation language for the component specs, any potential application builder will be able to understand, integrate, and extend the components. Furthermore, tool vendors have been easily able to integrate the components in their tool sets for modeling and code generation.

Enjoy!

Staffan Ahlberg   **Tomas Bräne**
CEO   **VP Research & Development**
IBS AB   IBS AB
www.ibs.se   *tomas.brane@ibs.se*

Preface

The excellent idea of writing a lightweight book on the Unified Modeling Language (UML) wasn't ours, we admit. This idea originated from Milan's customers. Having taught more than a hundred courses and seminars on component approaches to software development and on UML over the past few years, he was repeatedly asked for "UML made easy" for people who specify, buy, or manage complex software systems, yet don't program them. This demand seems logical given the way UML is being used in projects and read of in the success stories[1] – as well as the increasing specification workload in any knowledge industry (see Introduction). However, as we moved on into this book project, both of us became increasingly enthusiastic about the idea, as did Cambridge University Press (CUP). Luckily, a majority of our readers are quite familiar with CUP from their own (variety of) fields; so this book is likely to be seen as accessible in most senses of the word.

Any system specification can state requirements on functionality, usability, reliability, performance, and supportability, as well as legal and technical constraints where relevant. In UML projects, we start from a view of the business – its processes and activities – and move into functionality, increment-

---

[1] The Object Management Group (OMG) owns and upgrades the UML standard; visit *www.omg.org*.

ing all the remaining, nonfunctional, bullet lists as we go. These are then resolved later, during construction, rather than during specification. As stressed in the chapter on components as well as implied throughout the book, wherever we're on the scale between "buy" and "build," the specification work and business analysis just don't simply disappear. Even with an off-the-shelf system, we still specify our requirements, and we still need to understand the essence of all those UML diagrams.

To keep this book lightweight, we stay reasonably lightweight on the art of balancing the content of internal/technical UML views. This kind of balance is key down the road, that is, later on in a software development project. It requires modeling the right aspects in the appropriate diagram view at a right level of detail in the initial stage of a project. However, we chose to appeal to the reader's common sense by pointing out the natural boundaries between the process view, the use-case view, and the structural (or conceptual) view, with the strengths and limitations of each view. Neither a blueprint of a building nor one of a software system can show everything at once. Some drawings depict the walls and the roof, others electricity, and yet others heating, air conditioning, water, and drainage; that is, we separate the concerns. What is noteworthy is that people proposing buildings learn quickly to keep away (hide) electricity aspects from the exterior view and vice versa.

Standards and components are a *serious boost to productivity* in software. In our experience, however, these are more likely to be practiced when introduced in a step-by-step, nonacademic, and not too reserved manner, as outlined in this book. As an enterprise sets its mind on component reuse, all professionals from junior programmers to top management become involved and, consequently, need to be offered a brief guidebook within their frame of reference. So, for software specialists struggling to shift from a detailed code-based approach to the conceptual models of the software design and architecture, we recommend exploring UML beyond this lightweight version.

Acknowledgments

As mentioned in the Preface, many people have gradually made us realize the need for a lightweight book like this, thus indirectly pushing it through. Thanks to many people at the Object Management Group, Aonix-Select UK, Linsoft, Cell Network, Rational Scandinavia, IBS. Thanks to Marie-Louise Westerberg and Esa Falkenroth (Swedish Meteorological and Hydrological Institute), Leif-Åke Andersson (Swedish Customs/IT), Eva Backe (Integra Enterprise Systems), Anna Hermansson (Ericsson Telecom), Bjørn-Erik Willoch (Institute of Process Innovation, now CAP Management Consulting), Stanislav Mlynář CEO, LBMS Prague), Esa Rantanen (Sema Group), Annika Hansen-Eriksson (Royal Institute of Technology, now at Sema Group), and many others. For hints on knowledge enterprises, thanks to Peter Stevrin (associate professor, IT Management, Blekinge Institute of Technology) and Leif Edvinsson (Manager Intellectual Capital, at Skandia). For my blueprint thinking as well as the life-cycle aspect introduced in the earliest decades of systems development, thanks to my earlier employer, Michael A. Jackson. Thanks to Johan Wretö (Wreto.com) and Dennis Parrot (Select Software Tools, now at iPlanet) for interesting hints on teaching UML to others. Special thanks to Richard M. Soley (Chair and CEO, Object Management Group) for his enthusiasm and encouragement at an early stage, after the OMG day in Stockholm.

Finally, our publisher, Lothlórien Homet at Cambridge University Press, certainly deserves considerable thanks for keeping her humor throughout the process and for balancing the text skillfully between "practically nothing" and "impractically heavyweight" (also, Lothlórien more or less banned most of my favorite, extremely compact but neither tidy nor especially comprehensible stock phrases, so thanks on behalf of the readers, too).

Milan Kratochvíl

To all my friends and colleagues over the years, especially Steve Latchem, Dave Piper, Baz Maybank, Chris Simons, Adam Partridge, Dave West; to Lothlórien Homet, my brilliant publisher; and to all my super clients, without whom this book would not have been written.

Barry McGibbon

About the Authors

Milan Kratochvíl

A degree in Business & Administration and Data processing, Stockholm University.

Born in Prague, living in the dynamic silicon area around Stockholm-Kista (ranked by *Wired* as a global number 2).

Working since 1977 as an IT consultant, instructor, and writer in methodology; independent since 1989, focusing on areas where IT and knowledge-intensive business meet.

Taught far more than a hundred courses and seminars on a commercial basis for developers, managers, or buyers of complex systems. Published several articles, reports, congress papers on methodology and knowledge management. An initiator/catalyst and project leader of three experience-exchange pools with The Swedish Computer Society in Stockholm a few years ago.

Lessons learned: there are two things in this world you should reuse every day – jokes and components.

Barry McGibbon

Worked in the IT industry since 1966, gaining a wide variety of experience, ranging from programming through to holding senior management positions with leading computing services and product providers.

A consultant since 1985, with involvement in numerous major initiatives for significant enterprises in the United States, Europe, and the United Kingdom.

Provides advice and counsel on managing software development, methodologies, improvement strategies, capability evaluations, and quality management systems.

Lectures widely in the United States, the United Kingdom, and Europe. Author of *Managing Your Move to Object Technology: Guidelines & Strategies for a Smooth Transition,* published by SIGS Books Inc., and a contributor on *Component Based Software Engineering,* published by Addison-Wesley. Technical chairman for Europe's largest component and object technology conference and a series editor for Cambridge University Press.

How to Customize This Book

Most readers of this book suffer from a lack of time, so here's a guide on how you can focus on the key chapters relevant to your role.

Process owners, reengineers, and similar roles usually consider the topics of *Chapters 1 and 2* as the essence of a project, so you're advised to read those chapters thoroughly and browse through the rest.

End-user representatives or other roles involved in man-machine interaction (MMI), manuals, user training, user interfaces (UI), or interfaces to other systems are advised to focus on *Chapter 3*.

Domain experts are advised to concentrate on *Chapter 4* and to browse through *Chapters 3 and 5*.

Managers, project-plan coordinators, venture capitalists, headhunters, or PA people could read *Chapters 1, 2, and 3* quickly and focus on *Chapter 6*.

Others reading the book simply out of curiosity might want to browse through the art first, and then choose topics that interest them for a second iteration.

In general, those not interested in specific details can skip the footnotes and boxes.

Chapter 1
Introduction

Software – Yet Another Knowledge Industry

Knowledge industries such as electronics, space, pharmaceuticals, or software are special. On the surface, they're the hotly-argued-upon backbone of the new economy, a concept that's no longer new. In our opinion, it's the *approach* to business that makes the difference, rather than a company's niche or age. Some old-economy veterans, such as global-automation vendor ABB, have rapidly expanded their R&D initiatives and resources, employing many more IT specialists than many so-called new high-profile IT firms. IT provides a foundation to a variety of current business ideas, including customer-driven manufacturing where a web customer configures the product or even the software guiding an industrial robot in manufacturing the chosen customized product.

Obviously, knowledge industries are more special under the shell than at this slightly superficial mass-media/thematic level. On one hand, they have business processes similar to other industries but, on the other hand, production/operations is a small part of any business dominated by R&D and by marketing the know-how of that organization.

1

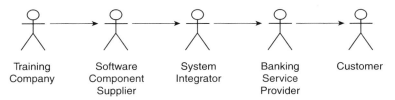

Figure 1-1 **A possible knowledge industry value chain.**

Awareness of knowledge-industry specifics is a project-time saver, both within the software industry itself and with the rapidly increasing number of its customers in the other knowledge industries. Knowledge industries are often interleaved with traditional industry sectors – today, you find computer chips and software in all the flagships of industrialism, from heavy trucks to railways. But, in a high-tech region, the complete knowledge-business value chain can sometimes grow remarkably long without any *tangible* ("hard") products whatsoever (Figure 1-1). For example, your customer might be a training company, whose customer is someone selling tools and methodology to a software house, some of whose customers provide Internet banking to e-traders, others providing sales configurators for customized insurance packages, and on it goes; sometimes, all the tangible hardware might seem to be produced on some other planet. Nevertheless, whichever the surrounding corporate culture or age of the enterprise, its IT parts must be considered a knowledge industry.

Classifying the Knowledge Industry

Figure 1-2 shows a kind of classification, pioneered 15 years ago by Karl-Erik Sveiby's team,[1] which makes us aware of the climate in our firm or project by starting from the extremes:

- A traditional *office:* a lack of real organization, of explicit common objectives, of know-how. Professor Parkinson's Laws apply. For example, an office of more than 150 employees doesn't need any external input because of generating its workload itself!

- A traditional *factory:* traditionally a hierarchy. Even in a modern factory, there's more focus on processes, work instructions/procedure

---

[1] Visit this Swedish-Australian writer and pioneer of knowledge management at *www.sveiby.com.au.* Books include *Managing Knowhow,* by Sveiby and Lloyd (Bloomsbury, London, 1997) and *The New Organizational Wealth,* by Sveiby (Berrett-Koehler, San Francisco, 1997).

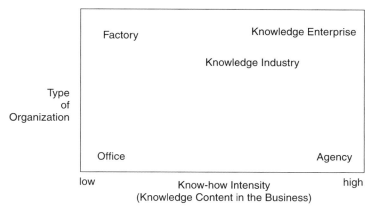

Figure 1-2 **Where is your corporate culture?**

steps than on creativity. In the past, the personnel were roughly supposed to take their hands with them in the morning – leaving their heads at home.

- An *agency:* creativity in an organizational chaos. Everyone is working hard and loves it – forgetting about surroundings, lunches, and colleagues. Anyone who becomes a burnout is considered an admirable role model.

- A *knowledge enterprise:* expertise combined with a common vision, structure, and cooperation. A knowledge enterprise solves complex problems of customers, while a service enterprise solves simple problems with appropriate repeatable procedures.

As you can see, no organization fits into any of the previous cartoons. The engine of the global economy is a gray zone that we prefer calling the knowledge industry: firms or projects that package their know-how into well-defined products and procedures, yet stay knowledge-intensive. Here, component-based approaches boosted by standards are the engine in most improvement efforts.

Consequences of the Knowledge Industry

Know-how intensity has some important practical consequences.

The production process becomes a *packaging machine* for the realization of the know-how, for example, the pharmaceutical factory for the know-how of R&D specialists. It must not fail, so all bottlenecks are banned, but these production costs are pennies compared to the acquisition and development of this know-how.

The silicon chip, the medical pill, the software CD, or the download-site is a *wrapper* for the know-how. We don't buy pills by weight. We pay for the expected improvement instead, no matter how it's packaged. Similarly, buying software by kilo-lines, (kLocs) of code doesn't make much sense. We pay for the expected business improvement, no matter the amount of new code or reused components. As the Object Management Group (OMG) points out, modern software projects avoid writing all the code for the programs. In other words, they reuse more infrastructure parts, off-the-shelf software components/business-oriented components than traditional projects do. In knowledge industries *know-how is the real thing,* whereas the wrapper is hardly relevant.

Unlike traditional mass production, the competitive edge isn't in the workflows of production/operations/administration, but in the mechanisms of *sharing and processing know-how* across the firm. Therefore, a traditional mechanical Business Process Reengineering (BPR) approach tends to solve the wrong problem when applied in a knowledge industry because it's focusing on the basic activities, without considering the complexity of the business logic in that activity.

The Asset Paradox

When the main asset of the firm is knowledge, then the trick is to stay fairly independent of individuals by turning a knowledge enterprise into a knowledge *industry.* This requires storing more knowledge in a format accessible to as many co-workers as possible, most often using computers. The labor market is simply a market. Therefore, even in a rather holistic bookkeeping approach, the (fancy) knowledge-asset figures must be adjusted by a factor reflecting their infrastructure, structuring, standardization, methodology, component-sharing, and so forth.

Acquiring and keeping unique knowledge is key in a clear-cut knowledge enterprise, whereas in a knowledge industry, the *structure* of the know-how – and the *infrastructure* used in keeping it current and in feeding it through – is as important as the know-how itself, a fact deserving attention from both knowledge managers and financial analysts.[2] Typically, a knowledge enter-

---

[2] Estimating/forecasting high-tech shares has been hotly argued since the 1980s. Focusing on knowledge structure and infrastructure is less fuzzy than trying to quantify pure knowledge. We hope to see less roller-coaster rides on NASDAQ in the future, as tech shares become less volatile when all such factors are thoroughly worked through and taken into account by analysts, ahead of IPOs or mergers. As we show in Chapter 6, configurable components can boost sales activities as well, by enabling a closer and cheaper match between bids and specific customer needs in a variety of niches.

prise *sells* knowledge, whereas a knowledge industry *sells its capability to apply and deploy its knowledge* packaged as, for example, software.

Sharing the Knowledge

Given all these specifics, the efficiency of specification and development activities is extremely important in any knowledge industry. The toolkit of improvement is all about knowledge sharing by:

- Standardizing the terms and the notation

- Practicing a common approach

- Sharing pretested components

UML has standardized the terms and the notation by providing a set of diagrams with a defined syntax. Unlike other knowledge industries, software can't be expressed by drawings or photographs of some spatial/physical, musical, biological, or chemical properties. Even under a fancy microscope, software stays *invisible and intangible.* A software-blueprint isn't as intuitive as a land map showing ice in white and water in blue. Rather, it presupposes a general industry-wide agreement in the first place, on the agreed meaning of every single symbol or relationship.

This makes us extremely dependent on a standard notation for any software-related communication and specification, all the way from a project developing a system from scratch to one selecting an off-the-shelf package. As development projects become increasingly global, UML also helps those of us communicating in our second or third language. For example, IBM development labs are located in dozens of countries, each with its own native language or languages, or the new Airbus Superjumbo involves industries from most of Europe. Atop of that, all natural languages include some natural ambiguity.[3] All things considered, word processors aren't enough as a tool of specifying requirements.

Practicing a common approach or method framework across projects, supported by a regularly upgraded knowledge aid, such as online mentors, built-in hyperbooks, or intelligent checks in a PC-based tool (a UML case tool), is knowledge sharing in a narrow sense. With cheap tools, we simply *access* the expert knowledge of others (typically, using standard search engines and hyperlinks) whereas, with automation tools, we can even *run* it

---

[3] A fact easily "rediscovered" while we're writing this book and asking others to read our first-draft text.

on a computer, and then simply access the results of the run (or let the computer use them), be it calculations or a more qualitative business logic.

We share pretested components across the firm and across the software industry. This kind of "canned know-how" from colleagues is a superior stage of knowledge sharing – we can activate the result right away, without ever acquiring the know-how that created it. This component that encapsulates the expert's knowledge and experience is kept up-to-date by the expert, leaving all the other developers free to concentrate on the business solution. This is an effective technique and a rather down-to-earth one when contrasted to preaching knowledge management at a thematic level. As we point out in the Chapter 6, this degree of automation can be increased further by smart configurator tools in the near future.

By and large, we encourage IT teams to exchange and adopt best practices from other sectors of industry. That said, we recommend *knowledge industries as sources* of ideas: many Business Process Reengineering cases and books described processes with a low-to-medium knowledge content, hardly applicable in the context of software specification and development. Although the bottom line might look deceptively similar, the devices and the activities generating that bottom line do differ, and those differences may be significant.

Sharing the Responsibility for Getting It Right

Even the buyer, the reengineer, or the process owner is involved in specifying and improving requirements throughout the project. In any knowledge industry, the customer and the vendor *share* this responsibility. Here, "the customer is always right" translates into "the customer always has the right to get the *right solution to the right problem.*" If you go to your car dealer and order a thirsty six-wheel-drive monster for driving from home to a job just around the corner, your dealer might laugh, as Figure 1-3 shows, but he offers and sells the monster to you anyway. On the other hand, if you try

Figure 1-3. **Some simple old approaches** to customer requirements don't count in a knowledge industry because a shared responsibility exists for the specification and its fit-for-purpose.

something similar in a knowledge industry, a serious vendor will raise strong objections on the mismatch between the business and your requirements because of this shared responsibility.

Sharing responsibility across the negotiation table involves *communication* at a pretechnical high level, as does sharing know-how within a team. Having combined rigor with easy-to-learn diagrams, UML has proven to be an excellent common IT language. UML is an unrivaled smorgasbord[4] of diagram ingredients matching a variety of needs. In business modeling, the stakeholder or the buyer works closely with the project team, gradually transferring work to the IT staff members as we move on (iterate) through the full system-development cycle.

A standard notation (or modeling language) greatly reduces ambiguity throughout the project.[5] This is important because ambiguity is a major source of confusion. You say the same thing, which is understood/reacted to in different ways by the listeners. For example, the clear statement "secure the building" will cause the Marines to form a taskforce and storm the building, a legal department to negotiate a long lease on the property, and the security experts to install and manage an access control system.

A good analogy exists on being multilingual. Milan speaks Swedish in Stockholm or Czech in Prague, just as you're fluent in your business language, be it in reinsurance, meteorology, switching, billing, or train control. Methodology experts or developers of a UML-tool understand UML at this level of detail, that is, all the diagrams' types, syntax, and rules. Milan can also speak a "standard language" – English – in frequent areas such as software, but not in areas like bug species (except software bugs of course).

Most software developers understand UML at this standard level.[6] UML resembles a grammatical language, such as Spanish or German, because of its predefined syntax and semantics. Nevertheless, we approach it in quite an idiomatic, example-based manner as common with today's English. With

---

[4] Usually translated as "Swedish table," a large table of ready-made dishes located in the middle of a restaurant, where the guests choose and pick their preferred combinations and quantities themselves, and then eat at their restaurant-tables.

[5] Language and reasoning are closely interrelated. As UML pioneer Dr. Ivar Jacobson points out, IT people used to think as humans until attending computer science classes at the university level, where they learn to think as computers (i.e., sequential Von Neumann machines splitting the world into data values and procedural instructions, which are poorly, or hardly, interrelated). UML provides the language necessary for reinventing the natural, human way of reasoning in the context of software systems. You can view it as a set of well-defined, preshrunk, standard mind maps that are useful to both the project team members and the software development tools to be used in the project.

[6] Typically, they also provide UML guidance to others throughout a project. The IIIE's list of software requirement qualities implies a cooperation here, stating that requirements shall be *unambiguous,* complete, correct, *consistent,* traceable, modifiable, *understandable,* verifiable, and *ranked* for importance and stability.

this language metaphor in mind, we found several good *Webster's* dictionaries are around for UML (addressing the "native"), as well as an extensive English course book or three (addressing the ambitious "guest scientist from abroad").

The missing link so far was a tour book on the language, accessible to many "frequent visitors" in the landscape of software projects. This tour book needs to fit in a lightweight cabin bag and be reasonably comprehensible, even during jet lags. From our customers, the pressure was on as well – so we wrote one.

Overconsumption of languages is excellent for brains, overconsumption of standard notations is far from excellent for a project approaching delivery deadline. With the smorgasbord principle in mind, let's pick up what we want and skip the cookies. If you're a software specialist, you'll soon read deeper books anyway.

Methods and Processes

UML standardizes the system documentation independent of how you produce it. Methodologies, on the other hand, are paths to take you from the problem to the solution and, during that journey, deliver the relevant UML diagrams.

UML provides diagram notations for most kinds of applications, so it works with all up-to-date methodologies, that is, with a component-based approach. Nevertheless, various practical methodologies are based on various ambitions and priorities. Some organize the overall problem-solving activities within a project – the cookbook approach – whereas others provide more how-to and the ingredients for the problem solver – the toolkit approach. Likely, this scale looks familiar to most readers who are specialists in non-IT areas. Of course, you can combine both ends of the scale in the same project: the UML notation works fine. Let's briefly compare three approaches in the following:

The Rational Unified Process™ (RUP)[7] makes the development process in a software project visible, from inception to deployment. Stressing, step by step, roles (30 kinds of "workers") and responsibilities for 60+ predefined

---

[7] from The Rational Corporation; visit *www.rational.com*.

BASIC STANDARDIZATION AND CREATIVITY BOOST EACH OTHER!

The recent standardization effort put into UML resembles trends from knowledge industries of the past. For centuries, classical music has been pushing its ubiquitous mix of science and creativity on a global market. We also find standard constructs in the American tradition, from a 12-bar blues to a jazz standard tune. Interestingly, when scaling-up sheer creativity into a knowledge industry, people always try to standardize the basics, to enable a shift of focus from low-level work to the big picture, that is, to *what we do* with the basics.

Unsophisticated music is as old as humanity itself. However, the "Big Art" music of the Western world emerged from extensive *standardization* only a couple of centuries ago. Before J. S. Bach, most churches used their own proprietary scales, some of which were impossible to play on instruments. Also, a tone could be pitched differently in different scales; thus, the same tone was played on different keys of the same keyboard. In cooperation with keyboard vendors, Bach pioneered *standard tempered scales* (major and minor, with standard tone intervals), enabling a leap in composer work and in interplay of instruments. A century later (W. A. Mozart and the classical period in music), common *architectural templates* already existed, such as a concerto in three movements (the slow one in the middle) or a symphony in four movements (the two slow ones in the middle, the latter of them a minuet.*) Similar architectural rules also governed the structure within each movement. A de-facto standard guided staging appropriate numbers of appropriate instruments in an orchestra, which gave the composer the necessary hints upfront in "design time," while composing the music – regarding the hardware to deploy the music later, onstage. As musicians were always borrowing-extending-reusing jerks and themes invented by someone else, even what we now call a *component approach* became frequent in the beginning of the classical period. For example, in large divertimentos, an evening or event was configured from a small "library" of ready-made components (movements). This greatly simplified and streamlined the requirement specification, yet matched the preferences of that particular evening's sponsor.

The long-term focus on Mozart in most creative professions** creates a major obstacle for a minority of programmers still trying to claim "no standards and no components, please – this is creativity." Long-term experience from other knowledge industries indicates exactly the opposite: extremely creative individuals benefit from architectural standards and components.

---

* To be exact, Mozart's Prague Symphony is the widely known exception to this rule because it omits the minuet movement (according to the BBC's "Best on Record," some 80+ recordings of the symphony exist worldwide).

** Many readers might remember Milos Forman's film *Amadeus* or Ingmar Bergman's *Magic Flute*, or several BBC documentary films on Mozart's music (among others). The creativity dimension was recently explored by Don Campbell in his book *The Mozart Effect* (Avon Books, 1997) and his CD-production, *Music for Creativity and Imagination* (Spring Hill Music®, 1997). In arguing that history repeats itself, we've also checked facts with Jiří Kratochvíl (Milan's father), a woodwind history expert at the Prague Academy of Music (see Pamela Weston: *Clarinet Virtuosi of Today*, Egon Publishers Ltd, 1989).

kinds of artifacts, RUP is a process framework suited for large projects, roughly of 70 members or more, with a large number of components to be constructed. RUP also outlines splitting the project into use-case-based (see Chapter 3) miniprojects, some running in sequence and some in parallel, in several iterations. Because RUP is distinctly use-case driven, some strengths and limitations of use cases affect the process itself. For example, a data warehouse/data mining or knowledge-based system implies hard work inside the system, despite rather simple external interaction, whereas use cases are easy to apply to telecom switching or to order handling, where a much larger proportion of external interaction (often with end users) takes place.

To a potential user of the process, we strongly recommend acquiring a thorough knowledge of UML to ensure the right aspects are dealt with in the right documents (artifacts). Providing guidelines from the requirement specification all the way to test, the process has become rather heavyweight, which implies some extensive process customization to start with to make the process fit the purpose. This customization needs to be done in two steps: first, for the enterprise, and second, for the project. In some 4,000+ web pages, this process framework defines roles, artifacts, work flows/activities, and project management.

IBM's WebSphere® Business Components,[8] an application framework previously known as the SF (for San Francisco or Shared Frameworks) is, on the other hand, a wholly *component-driven* approach. IBM supplies off-the-shelf, pretested components, books, best practices, and instruction to solution suppliers who target customers requiring e-business, CRM, and ERP packages. Thus, SF is a component *framework* for application projects – large or small ones – typically employing more reused pretested components than new ones. SF motivates the doers rather directly: here we have a box of software Lego bricks and the directions for use, so let's go ahead.

SF's strengths and limitations are typical of a specialist's method. Such methods are precustomized for certain systems – in SF's case, the closer to ERP/CRM/e-business, the more useful it is. We hope similar complete frameworks will also emerge in some other niches. By shrinking development timescales, SF guides projects into smooth construction work: more assembly, less programming. As senior developers at Swedish ERP-vendor IBS[9] as well as their R&D Manager and Vice President Tomas Bräne points out, having found a couple of appropriate SF components, a day might sometimes be enough to develop a sophisticated "new" one.

---

[8] from the IBM Corporation; visit *www.ibm.com/software*.

[9] At the end of 2001, IBS is ranked third in the world by AMR Research, and Frost & Sullivan in the field of supply chain management (visit *www.ibs.se*).

Aonix's Select Perspective™[10] is a balanced component-based approach in the middle of the previous scale. It fits medium and large projects using a medium-to-large proportion of pretested, internally developed (and owned) components. Along with that, Aonix suggests employing IBM's SF components off-the-shelf, whenever appropriate. Guidance is delivered by books, instruction, and an interactive manual (Process Mentor) integrated in Perspective's UML-toolkit, the Select Component Factory. An object repository is used to keep track of, cross-reference, and manage both project documents and common enterprise ones *(cross-project),* large or small. For example, if phone-no is used in 20 components and we have to add three digits to it for country codes, we alter only once. A practical interplay of component management and application development is stressed throughout. Select Perspective's range is wider than SF's and narrower than RUP's: enterprise systems in finance, government, administration, airlines. Select Perspective shrinks the development process, aligns requirements to business processes, *and* enables more assembly from components with less programming and with improved delivery times.

As you can see, people use UML in a variety of approaches. An enterprise can easily put together a customized approach, based on one or more common process-frameworks. The OMG is currently coordinating the development of a Software Process Engineering standard (SPE) with the longer-term objective of providing interoperability across tools and formats (repositories) in the software process-engineering field.[11]

Whichever your firm's variant, make sure both systematic *component management* and continuous *component development* processes are alive and well. They deserve the same priority as in other sectors of industry because future reduction in costs and lead time, with improved quality and flexibility, justifies this initial investment. Therefore, we stress the component approach throughout this book and focus on components in the final chapters.

Summary

Knowledge industry, including software, is special in many ways. The responsibility for a good specification is shared across the negotiation table, thus creating a need for high-level, pretechnical communication. Because software is intangible, we rely on well-known diagrams with a standardized notation. Standards and components are a great boost to any knowledge

---

[10] from Select Business Solutions of Aonix *www.aonix.com.*

[11] Visit *www.omg.org/techprocess/meetings/schedule/SPE_Management_RFP.html.*

industry, from extremely old and up to dotcom. Even a basic knowledge of how to communicate in UML can prevent considerable ambiguity and mis-understanding in a project.

The original influences on the UML standard were rather diverse, result-ing in a kind of smorgasbord of ingredients that the enterprise can cus-tomize quite easily to fit its needs. At the moment, the field of software development processes isn't as standardized as the UML notation. Process standardization efforts are underway within the OMG. This work will take time, however, but the big leap toward a standard notation has already been taken and the UML works fine with any up-to-date development process.

Chapter 2
Aligning to the Business

Before modeling the design of the system, a project team typically models the business processes to identify the scope of the planned system and to ensure that any chosen system aligns to the demands of both this business model and business vision.

A variety of possible diagram techniques exist for delivering this business model, as well as possible levels of ambition. With business redesign, a risk occurs of having eyes for nothing else but the modeling and ignoring some real dangers. The hard work isn't about creating a best-of-breed business model; it's about enforcing corporate change within the organization. To remind the reader of these risks, we've made separate box diagrams of the more fancy UML features. Here, lengthy modeling exercises might become a convenient excuse for avoiding challenge and confrontation with the permafrost layers found in many organizations. This challenge and lack of confrontation is a common pitfall in implementing new business practices. Therefore, process innovation methodologies spend little time analyzing the current (as is) processes – often, a quick diagnosis is enough. Instead, we focus on the new business models: the business to be.

Ownership of the business models must remain with the stakeholders and process owners. This avoids the danger of the new processes being seen as the work of the IT department, which can lead to rejection of the models by the process owners. It must be made clear that the IT specialists act only as *agents* in producing the business models.

Most business modeling methodologies try to structure activities, that is, the everyday *dynamics* of a business. Others recommend using both dynamics and structure in early business modeling. All things considered, we always stress the view matching the nature of our business in a project, trying out both dynamic and structural paths in a low-ceremony (quick) approach, and then pushing forward through the most promising one.

In a knowledge-intensive process where a lot of knowledge is dispersed in an unstructured form and held in many persons' heads, forgetting about traditional industries and starting from structure and know-how is worthwhile. These are represented in class diagrams, knowledge assets, business rules, and so forth. We can eliminate most work flows early by aiming at an automated one-stop shop solution. As the UML provides a smorgasbord originating from several sources, its notation works fine with a variety of approaches and priority objectives, as shown in Figure 2-1.

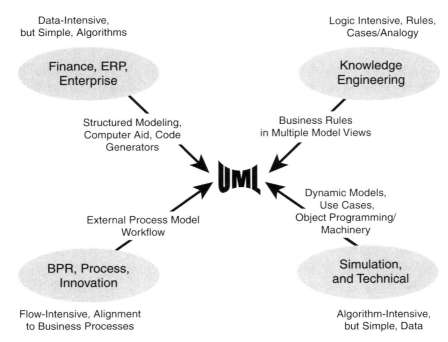

Figure 2-1. **UML's smorgasbord** – ingredients originating from several fields and appealing to a couple of fields each.

For example, when modeling a help desk for complex products, a traditional process model might show that each help-desk issue takes a carousel ride through the enterprise, visiting the desktops of various specialists until the issue is resolved. A structural approach, on the other hand, would stress call avoidance instead, using computers to execute frequently used know-how to resolve issues automatically, passing only exceptions to the human-in-the-loop. In hi-tech industries, e-help desks are a good example of this knowledge-oriented approach.[1] Case bases being its simplest kind, *adaptive* technology combines with the Web into an extremely powerful tool of business automation. Where feedback of know-how from new real-world cases is provided by thousands of web users, the system's capability to resolve new kinds of daily business problems will follow a steep learning curve, most often keeping the whole support process a simple man-machine dialogue in a semi-natural language.

With the process approach, two kinds[2] of business process models can be provided in the UML:

- Activity diagrams
- Business use cases, an extension to UML

Using UML Activity Diagrams

Like other process-flow approaches, UML activity diagrams show the complete chain of activities for a single process. When there are many processes, we recommend that the activity diagrams be complemented by some kind of a graphical index of processes, for example, a simple, top-down process hierarchy chart or a simple business use-case diagram.

Strengths
This *process-flow* modeling technique fits long/complex back-office process chains, where other systems might be involved in addition to our system-to-be and sometimes also interleaved with manual activities. If that sounds like your project, then modeling the business process flows is what we recom-

---

[1] For an example of a case-based automated help desk, see Ask Iris Online.™ Ask a question, in plain English, and Iris will try to answer it using a Toshiba knowledge base. *www.csd.toshiba.com*

[2] You might want to investigate other alternatives further:
  - Other process-flow notations (Catalyst, FirstSTEP, and so forth). The Workflow Management Coalition also has a cross-tool standard Process Definition Language. PC-tools are around, some of them supporting process simulation, what-if questions, and various resource-utilization/product/efficiency analyses.
  - T. Winograd's Action-Workflow approach, top-down cycle-style.
  - M. A. Jackson's structure-influenced approach.

mend. Existing organization and software is often put in question and reshaped as a result of this process analysis.

Limitations

Activity diagrams are usually less suited for *knowledge-intensive* activities, however, where flows are a perfect solution for the wrong problem. They are also less suited for front-office (e-) activities where the customer clicks/jumps more freely across processes, thereby turning our business process redesign into event-driven dialogue design, whether we like it or not.

Because a picture is worth a thousand words, we have shown several examples of business process models using UML-activity diagrams:

1. Drinking in Florida

2. Drinking in Prague

3. Drinking in Stockholm

4. Drinking in 2080

Drinking in Florida

Figure 2-2 shows the basic thirst-slaking process for any business intending to stay in the sun, for example, Florida.

With the variety of paths offered under a variety of circumstances [conditions], the benefits of diagramming the flow become visible. The icons in an activity diagram are simply activities performed by people, machines, or both. Most often, we focus on activities and postpone (or skip) issues like who will be doing what (see the box on p. 18).

As you can see in Figure 2-2, an activity can even have multiple exits, labeled by [conditions] (see Ask for a Soft Drink). It can have multiple entries, interpreted in an OR manner: the activity is simply triggered, no matter which way it has been currently entered, as is the case with Pay. Conditional paths might even be shown explicitly by decision nodes (see the box on p. 20).

The horizontal bars, called *synchronization bars,* start and end *parallel activities,* which is a major point in any process redesign. For example, to improve lead time, we either remove an activity or choose to perform it in parallel with other activities.

From this point of view, most old procedures were excessively sequential, which can be diagnosed from a bar shortage in the activity diagram. Where drawn at all, the as-is diagram version often grows to a rather unstructured, wallpaper-sized sketch, so we usually skip it.

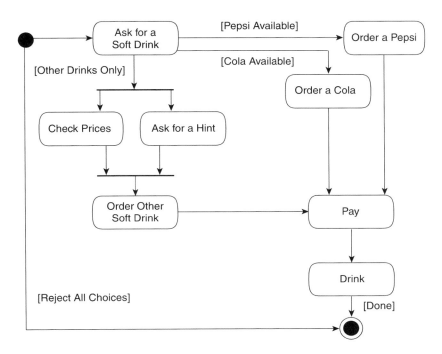

Figure 2-2. **Drinking in Florida**

Drinking in Prague

Figure 2-3 shows a thirst-slaking business process in Prague where "one XL size fits all."

In Prague, for the last thousand years or so, native pub customers have always expected only beer.[3] This has resulted in a remarkably simple workflow. In some pubs for locals, taking a seat makes an appropriate number of pints (half-liters) emerge automatically on the guests' table, without an explicit order – a true *management-by-exception* style. You drink the beers placed before you, and then, in time refuse any more beers. No explicit order occurs because entering the pub (a business event[4]) translates into an implicit one.

Figure 2-3 shows that where an activity is entered once and repeated

---

[3] Proving that reducing customer uncertainty by offering standardized products was practiced centuries ahead of the current global trademarks and brand marketing!

[4] You'll discuss events often when producing activity diagrams. They are the key triggers to all main processes.

SWIM LANES

Where "who does what" is important, some projects prefer a layout consisting of several parallel swim-lane partitions within each activity diagram (see Figure B2-1). Lines show the lane boundaries – with one department, person/role, or software component responsible for each lane. This adds the dimension of *responsibility* and exposes "hand overs" between different groups, which often causes process problems.* Most UML tools support lanes.

In our experience, this is a later step because ahead of responsibility issues, the initial activity diagrams must capture the "what" and "what order" of the proposed business process. If we try to start from responsibility instead, we often get stuck in old vertical organization models and their functional, non-process ways of thinking. In addition to this mental trap, many organizational units or automated software components responsible for the proposed activities still remain to be specified and designed down the road. *Processes are horizontal* and cross-department, so process redesign typically postpones the issue of responsibility. The typical course of steps here is customer-value/process objective – order of activities – responsibility. Also, all these steps show how important it is for the business experts and the process owners to become closely involved at this stage.

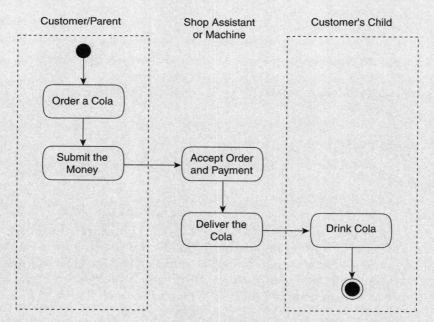

Figure B2-1. **Swim lanes.** With thirsty children or teenagers, a cola-order process can be partitioned into three swim lanes, showing each responsibility partition.

---

* With parallel workflows, the communication between the threads is more restricted in the UML than what is common elsewhere in "flow" style diagrams.

many times, it is modeled as *one* icon with an asterisk symbol (as is the case with Drink), and then terminated by an arrow with a condition saying something like [Refuse another one] or [No more left].

Here, the management-by-exception style leads to a greatly simplified business process. This process simplification is common in full-scale projects as well. Flow models, such as activity diagrams, tend to evolve into rather simple ones as a result of process redesign – as some activities become superfluous, some are merged, and some are automated. This example also illustrates another common problem, however, as extreme process-optimization introduces the risk of tunnel vision, translating into long-term costs somewhere else. In this example, the long-term costs are certainly transferred to the health care sector.

As you can tell from the [Beer sold out] condition, modeling rare error handling isn't relevant because those can be taken care of manually, alongside/outside this process. For the first version of an activity diagram – and of any dynamic model – make sure to target only mainstream scenarios, that is, the basic course, the happy path, the golden case, and so forth. Where necessary at all, extra detail is introduced in the next version. Here, we made such an addition, marking it as a dotted line. In our experience, such additions emerge from security and control issues, rather than from the primary objective of the process.

Figure 2-3 shows the basic drinking process in this streamlined kind of a

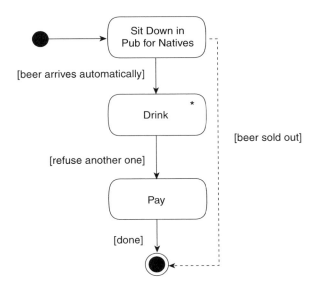

***Figure 2-3.* Drinking in Prague.**

DIAMONDS MIGHT NOT BE YOUR BEST FRIEND!

UML even allows diagrams showing decisions as explicit nodes (empty diamond icons) (see Figure B2-2). But, in practice these lead to lengthy discussions on gray-zone decision activities. For example, a decision step that includes work, like searching for and fetching the things to be decided on, such as beverages, is an activity and needs to be described as such. Therefore, if a project is pedantic on decision nodes, the size of the diagram tends to double. Remember, the meaning of the model is exactly the same even without the explicit decision nodes, that is, with arrows drawn directly from the preceding activity icon.

Clutter (rather than glitter) in the diagram is the smaller problem. The bigger problem is the time spent discussing those gray-zone steps that some team members view as an activity and others see as a decision. That's why we skip the diamonds in Figure B2-3.

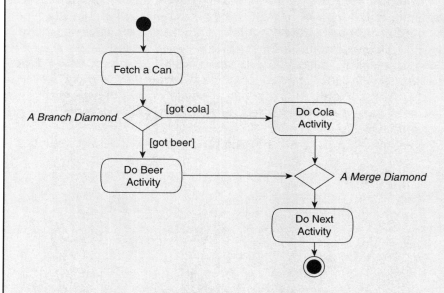

Figure B2-2. Decision nodes separated. All that glitters is not diamonds.

(continued)

Prague pub. This order and consumption process can be complemented by the matching supply process: a waiter waiting for the customer, opening the next barrel, pouring the beers, serving tables until an order is refused, collecting payment, tidying the table. This might introduce the concepts of waits (see the Dangerous Waits box on p. 22), as it is important to show other waiter activities when they're waiting for customers.

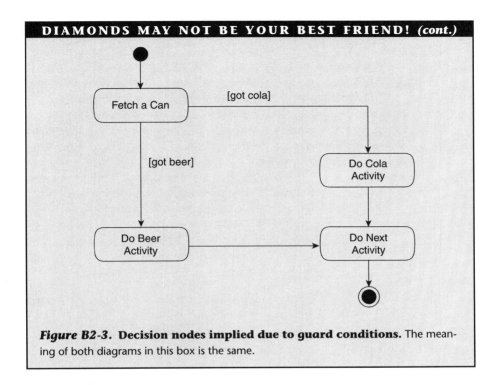

DIAMONDS MAY NOT BE YOUR BEST FRIEND! *(cont.)*

Figure B2-3. **Decision nodes implied due to guard conditions.** The meaning of both diagrams in this box is the same.

Drinking in Stockholm

Figure 2-4 shows a future thirst-slaking process demanded in the past by some humoristic students in Stockholm.[5] Suppose the customers are being connected directly to the brewery, then the complex flow of process steps is replaced by the rather literal flow of liquid to the customer.

This is an innovative process redesign, illustrating at the same time the limitation of activity diagrams and flow models. With a high degree of automation and self service, lengthy work flows *collapse* into only an activity or three. So, as the activity-diagram exercise nears completion, the diagram itself tends to disappear.[6] Ideally, the process modeling might deliver

---

[5] A practical joke by a couple of students at The Royal Institute of Technology in Stockholm, Sweden, was the purchase of only one stock share in Stockholm's largest brewery. Since then, they've attended every annual meeting of shareholders, proposing repeatedly a large *pipeline* across the city *to connect the brewery directly to the school* (a "major customer to-be").

[6] This is a simple order-process example, but a high degree of automation has also been tested with knowledge technologies in other processes. For example, the brewing process in North America, by Beck's Brewery *(www.becks.de)*.

THE DANGEROUS WAITS

In a flow model, like an activity diagram, it's practical to indicate *waits* because challenging them is the point of the whole exercise. If an insurance policy, for example, takes four weeks to complete, while total active time, with our insurance people working on it, is only four minutes, then we obviously need a new, more straightforward business process. If we're in luck, we get rid of the wait in the final process version. If we're unlucky – as the cause of the wait might be beyond our control – we mark it visually, to target it in the future.

Furthermore, by examining these wait points and asking "what happens if the expected event doesn't happen?" usually uncovers new functionality and requirements for the planned solution. In our insurance example, an obvious question is "what happens if the policy isn't completed in time?" Are there penalties? is it no longer legal? can we sue someone? are customer claims valid? and so forth.

an almost-empty diagram of the process-to-be, replacing a wallpaper-sized process-as-is, and resulting in some jokes about what management consultants are paid for. However, this is a logical consequence of the objective to accomplish more by less ("less is more").

Business automation also results in increased complexity within the system. This is prevalent when attempting to model processes involving customers' use of the Web. Web-based knowledge processing offers a shift from zigzag work flows to a one-stop shop that makes the process model look rather brief. This is caused by complex *business logic* – recently performed by people – moving from the outside to the inside of the system and, thus, turning business complexity into system complexity which needs to be modeled in other kinds of UML diagrams. Remember, the *complexity is still there*, except for some redundant activities being eliminated, but now, it's encapsulated *within* the future system.

Drinking in 2080

Imagine a new company called Wet-Liquids.com that delivers drinks to subscribers in smart houses in the year 2080 – a *future* thirst-slaking business. E-beer/e-cola can be downloaded on request to registered drinkers with payment made against drinks consumed. If this sounds too futuristic, then think of download-on-demand books or music instead, where this distribution channel is already being used. Otherwise, just suppose our firm of 2080 has several e-brewing patents pending that connect the Net

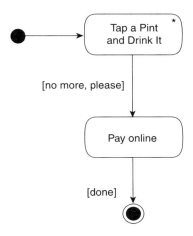

Figure 2-4. Drinking in Stockholm. The flow of process steps has been replaced by a literal flow of liquid to the customer.

to water pipes, applying a kind of telecom package-switching technology to liquids.[7]

Old, semi-manual work flows have disappeared because of extensive automation. Business process logic has become system logic, which simplifies our business model and makes activity diagrams less useful. We need another way to express the business view. This is when Jacobson's *business use-case diagrams* are more appropriate for specifying requirements for such highly automated systems.

Using Business Use-Case Diagrams

Business use-case diagrams emphasize value added and roles, called business actors and business workers, thus sharing some strengths and limitations with use cases (see Chapter 3). Generally speaking, a use case can be explained in detail in a description of the sequence of activities. For example: customer selects type of drink, system checks if valid request (depends on subscription

---

[7] According to some European newspapers, The Coca-Cola Company is about to test a prototype cola distribution through the water supply system in New York. Test households then literally add the company's *essence* to carbonated water. However, according to The Coca-Cola Company, that prototype - doesn't exist. If this is a practical joke by a news agency, we think it's a good one and let it reappear in 2080 because, although appetizing in flow models (as shown), beverages are far from a hi-tech commodity yet. On the other hand, it's a *commonly known* one. Unlike hi-tech products, this commodity also permits book examples to stay futuristic, yet lightweight (roughly, the opposite of regular frequenters).

and type of drink), system either dispenses drink or refuses request. If the sequence is too complicated and involves waits, and so forth, then an activity diagram offers more expressive power than a business use case.

Strengths

Business use cases typically fit front office (e-) activities with external inter-actions where external business actors, such as customers or suppliers, tend to skip across processes as they want. Where this is the case, we might need to structure the dependencies between processes, sometimes borrowing even standard use-case relationships from the next chapter.

When published several years ago, business use cases met much less enthusiasm than Ivar Jacobson's use cases did in general. Customers were modeled as end users of a business, but this user relationship becomes rather literal as businesses make web sites their front offices. A new niche for the technique is thus emerging from a gray zone between traditional business modeling and standard use cases.

Limitations

This technique alone doesn't visualize long back-office style process chains. If these seem important to our project, we stress business process flows and we use activity diagrams.

Also, in a knowledge-intensive business, this technique is a starting point – not *the* point. Under such circumstances, we have to express business rules and constraints early or derive them by information-mining techniques, such as rule induction, or capture real cases in a case base. In businesses with high knowledge content, standard mainstream modeling tends to solve peripheral problems and avoid facing the challenge of describing the knowl-edge itself.

Figure 2-5 shows the four business use cases for Wet-Liquids.com. Each use case corresponds to a business process that might develop into a larger system use-case structure. This can even work without an activity diagram – as all activities are moved into our e-business system. This is an example of the gray zone between business-process modeling and standard use cases. Here, the technique is accepted as natural by most people.

In Figure 2-5, a business actor called "Customer" (stick person icon) par-ticipates directly in one business use case at a time, maybe using a graphical menu.[8] Use-case icons with a slanting line denote the *business* use cases,

---

[8] Even in the past, however, with customers typically serviced by middlemen's hands (i.e., by front-office personnel), the diagram would look the same. The customer is viewed as the end user of the busi-ness process.

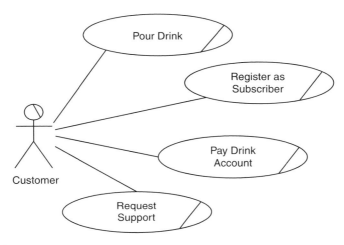

Figure 2-5. **Drinking in 2080.**

whereas system use cases don't have the slash. No matter what the notation, we recommend you model use cases in two levels of detail to avoid a split of focus: the business level and the system level.

With this kind of dialogue structures and interdependencies, use-case modeling (the next step is covered in Chapter 3) is a practical technique in the dialogue with analysts or system designers.

But What About the Data?

We have several reasons to keep data modeling short in this lightweight book. As we explain in Chapter 7, data modeling is a technique suitable later on in the development process and, in addition, it has been covered thoroughly for decades.[9] Also, in UML, we typically model *both* information *and* what the system will be doing with it. This is shown in the structural view (see Chapter 4).

---

[9] However, at this stage (the process model), some people list the assets needed by the process: person-nel, machinery, raw materials/hardware components, knowledge/business rules, and even information, including the inputs and outputs to the process (typically, by simply referring to existing ones – at this stage, we're concerned with the main items, such as personal details). Using a repository (a database of UML definitions) this can be done by cross-referencing the relevant parts of the process-model view and their corresponding parts in the structural view.

Summary

Unsurprisingly, when aligning to business, we start with a business model, consisting of up to three views:

- *The process-flow view.* UML activity diagrams mirror the course of activities in a flow, stressing the structure of a particular process. As the process innovation or automation exercise nears completion, they might collapse to near zero.

- *The e-view.* Business use-case diagrams mirror a set of (sometimes automated) procedures, some of which can be shown in detail in activity diagrams. As the focus is on several processes, they can be useful where e-customers use the business in an ad-hoc manner, frequently crossing process boundaries. In most methodologies, we continue from business use cases into standard (system) use cases (see Chapter 3).

- *The knowledge view.* A third, structural view becomes necessary where the domain is complex or knowledge intensive or the processes are too simple. The structural view is provided by class diagrams (see Chapter 4). We often need to add rules or case bases to this view.

Chapter 3

Adding Rigor
to the Requirements

*B*usiness modeling concerns process owners, reengineers, or business analysts with IT specialists in an advisory role. Later, in class modeling and especially in object interaction modeling, IT people become the driving force. Here, in adding rigor to the requirements through use-case modeling, there's a shared effort. Business experts provide the essence of the requirements, while IT specialists provide the structure. Having modeled the business, we now start aligning the system specification – most of it being the functional requirements – to the requirements of our business processes.

A diagram technique for this is very widespread: UML standard use cases that were pioneered some 20 years ago by Ivar Jacobson. *Use cases* are simply the ways in which the actors use the system. A similar step is natural in *any* knowledge industry because exact requirements minimize lead time and misunderstandings.

Use Cases

Human-computer interaction (HCI) is a vast field, to which use cases contribute with a practical, down-to-earth technique for the doers. To end users of the planned solution, the user interface often seems to be the entire system. Use cases extend this simplified view by modeling what's going to happen at the user interface, as well as interfaces to other systems. Use cases, interface layout examples, and prototypes complement each other, so they fully define the functional requirements of the system. Any remaining UML diagrams specify the inside/kernel of the system hidden behind that interface. The expectations to be met are similar in all three of the use cases, layouts, and prototypes:

- Users need to rely on/feel comfortable with the system.

- The HCI feels easy, yet not boring, and it matches both common standards and the user's view of the business activity.

Sometimes, one use case can involve multiple forms of user interface. For example, in a management game, all these kinds of views might be available in parallel, as separate windows or as several partitions of the same window in a use case like "Your next move." For example, the views may include a world map, 3-D movie shots, diagrams of results, and a control panel with sliders for allocating/increasing/decreasing investment to various areas. Also, a web-dialogue use case, such as e-purchase, can span four or five form pages in only one use case, which isn't completed until the last page has been successfully submitted into the system.

Functional requirements are expressed in this UML use-case model, whereas the nonfunctional requirements are recorded in supplementary text, such as separate e-documents,[1] or as footnotes to UML documents.

Requirement elicitation takes considerable cooperation in brainstorming, workshops, interviews, storyboarding, and prototype evaluation. Use cases work fine as long as you use them to specify functionality as *external interactions* in the right place: the system boundary. This takes some experience and common sense, so we provide "warnings" toward the end of this chapter.

Strengths

More than any other technique, use cases make external interaction requirements clear, including their interdependencies. This provides an answer to the challenge of many, complex, or important external interactions. For example, those for mobile phones, switching, booking, or incoming orders. Use cases simplify some additional activities, such as project management, mentioned in the section "Use-Case Example."

---

[1] We use the term "e-documents" throughout to indicate those documents produced by the varieties of word processors and in various formats, including HTML.

Limitations

Sophisticated systems hide a complex interior behind a surprisingly simple exterior. For example, on icy roads, drivers don't expect a complex user dialogue from antiskid systems and stabilizers, but they do expect stability and survival to be delivered automatically. With knowledge systems, data warehouse, or data mining, standard use cases can only provide a sketchy starting point, rather than the expected hints about our system-to-be. Sometimes these starting points are as simple as Start, Stop, Repeat. Furthermore, in complex agent/batch processing, systems often behave like (human) actors: rather than being driven by external interactions, they can be self-driven by internally generated events. In all similar cases, you need to specify the structure of your system-to-be early on in the project to get a realistic picture.

Why do we have rather general expressions like "actors" and "use cases"? One reason is the practical convenience of a brief, well-defined term. An *actor* covers *both* "a person like a user or system administrator" and "an external system interacting with our system-to-be." Similarly, a *use case* – "a behaviorally related sequence of interactions, performed by an actor with the system" – covers a variety of external interactions, from a user dialogue to a stepwise handshake between two software systems without humans in the loop.

Before we start to identify the use cases, we list all actors supposed to be in touch with the system boundary. The list makes it easier to determine the use cases required by these actors. Jacobson's original Swedish term (*aktör,* with a double-dot above the *o*) corresponds to "actor" in a market-like context, rather than on stage. Typically, an actor has a well-defined role within a business and some of the actor's business activities become use cases in our system-to-be. For example, in a system specification for a theater, UML actors are payroll clerks, producers, marketing personnel, external travel agency systems, and so forth.[2] Any actor can be involved in a single use case, or several use cases, with or without other actors, as we can see in Figure 3-1.

Use-Case Example

In the business example for Drinking in 2080 in Chapter 2 (Figure 2-5), we saw business use cases for downloading drinks and providing some online support. As we look into the business use case called Request Support, the resulting use cases for the system (called *system use cases*) turn out to be web-customer dialogues, as shown in Figure 3-2. The core is a mainstream system use case, which is often outlined quite *explicitly* by the process-owner or reengineer.

From this mainstream system use case, others appear in the structure

---

[2] They take part in system dialogues, rather than Shakespearean dialogues.

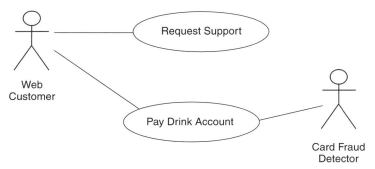

Figure 3-1. **A system use case** can be related to several actors, as is the case in Pay Drink Account. An actor can be related to several use cases, as is the case with Web Customer.

linked by use-case relationships (the dashed arrows in the diagram). These related use cases – let's call them *mini-use cases* – represent complementary activities that are either *less usual* or *common* interactions *reappearing* in other use cases. These mini-use cases and their relationships are usually modeled by the IT staff, so for other stakeholders in the project, the ability to read and understand the arrows will do.

In use-case relationships, the dashed arrows show the dependency and a «stereotype» denotes a variant (this time, a variant of that dependency). Thus, the *«include» arrow* between the use cases makes the mainstream use case *always include* the mini-use case, that is, it's dependent on that use case. To get online support on our Web site, customers must confirm product

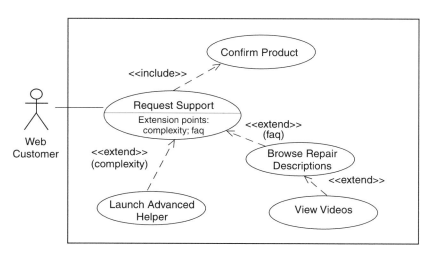

Figure 3-2 **System use cases for online support.**

GENERIC ACTORS

UML also supports *abstract* (generic) actors,* such as "someone doing the bookings" or "customer contact personnel." Although not widespread, this simplifies both vendor specifications for off-the-shelf software packages and enterprise systems that must be adjusted to many local branches. For example, if you intend to sell a booking and scheduling package to anyone from dentists to lawyers (as in Figure B3-1), the specification can't rely on actor definitions from a single sector of industry. Therefore, we prefer a few abstract actors to start with for the use cases, rather than an ever-growing list of "real" actors.

You can even let a single ("abstract") stick figure generalize several roles in the *same* business as long as it's involved in the same dialogues.

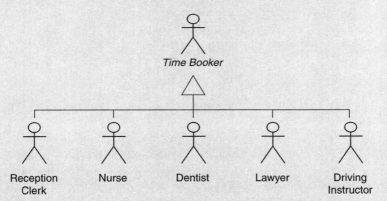

Figure B3-1. An abstract actor represents several kinds of actors – often from several business units – all of these using the system in the same way and playing the same role in, for example, the booking dialogue. This technique comes in handy where appropriate, although it is seldom used.

---

* Abstract actors have their names put in italics.

details. This mini-use case can now be shared by several mainstream use cases, not only in support, but also in marketing or delivery planning. If this mini-use case were made part of the mainstream, then the result would be doubled maintenance in the future because changes to the product-confirmation mini-dialogue would be repeated in all those mainstream use cases.

The *«extend» arrow* between use cases makes the mainstream use case pointed to *sometimes extended by* the one pointing to it. A condition will be stated later on, referring to an extension point stated under the horizontal line in the mainstream use case – for example, the extension point called *complexity.* Another example:

- If a possible repair is found, the customer can browse the information and also view any relevant videos (another «extend»).

- If no repair is found, then the advanced helper is used to assist in defining the problem.

Everyone needs some guidelines on reading the arrows here: unsurprisingly, we always read in an arrow's direction. Read the diagram once again if you want.[3] Thus, the «extend» arrows point the opposite way (*to* the mainstream icon) because we parse them in their direction. Here. for example, we want the (rare) Launch Advanced Helper mini-use case to extend the mainstream one.

Because business experts or process owners prioritize the mainstream use cases before the detail is added, most of these included and extending use cases are discovered and defined by IT people as use-case analysis proceeds. However, if we just *list* only the apparent ones among these mini-use cases early for resolution later – simple footnotes in the mainstream description will do – we'll save time down the road. Again, the process owner provides the *essence* here, the IT staff provides the *structure,* and a mutual dialogue adds detail.

The result is a focused, structured, semi-formalized requirement specification, beyond the expressive power of plain text. Some technology zealots get bored by this unsophisticated work but, in any knowledge industry, a well-thought-through specification saves considerable time. So, a project manager must carry on with use cases and let such individuals program a sketchy prototype instead. This *prototype* gives a facade that "fakes" the events for some use cases, without having the real system in place. This confirms our interpretation of the specification.

Static layout prototypes like screens, windows, and web pages are a perfect supplement to use cases as use cases focus on the traffic (of transactions, signals, and so forth) passing through the layout into our future system and out from it. A layout visualizes only the *look* of the system boundary, whereas a use case describes a *course of events* expected there.

Use cases help define the distinct system boundary early on in the project, which is shown as the large rectangle enclosing the use cases.[4] This

---

[3] By the way, many first-cut use-case models tend to have an arrow or three pointing the wrong way. This would make maintenance difficult because we're unlikely to know the details several months, or years, later.

[4] In a complex solution where a number of systems might be communicating with each other, sometimes it's useful to show a rectangle for each system (often called a "domain") and the dependencies between use cases in different domains (for example, an activity diagram, a business use-case diagram, or a high-level sequence diagram, mentioned in Chapter 4).

UML USE-CASE GENERALIZATION

A third kind of relationship applies when a use case provides a new "special" *variant* of the mainstream one. A few steps can be added (that *resembles* «extend») and some other steps are changed (this makes a difference because we alter rather than simply complement a predefined course of events). Suppose you provide a special support dialogue on our web site where customers get free support regarding our competitors' products. This dialogue is only partly similar to the general mainstream one (same as . . . , *except* . . .), as we can see in Figure B3-2. For example, this dialogue can be decorated with tempting ad banners (promoting our products instead) and some spiteful comments by a sharp and humorous cartoonist. So, although the customer objective is the same in both dialogues, some steps leading there still differ. As we can see in this dialogue, the definition of intent (or business value) tends to double where we're going to deal with direct e-customers. For example, where a customer intent (bug-fixing) might be different from an enterprise intent (additional sales in the future to beat a competitor) – both of them in the *same* use case.

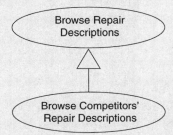

Figure B3-2. Use-case generalization. Here, we've joined them to beat them.

early identification of the system boundary speeds the decisions on what's provided by users, by other systems (external and, therefore, modeled as actor icons), and by use cases of our system-to-be.[5]

For Project Managers, use cases become useful in project planning and monitoring. Stakeholders of the project – business managers, process owners, and so forth – prioritize the use cases based on their importance or value to the business. In the example in Figure 3-2, the top priority is for Request Support (the mainstream), Confirm Product, and Browse Repair Descriptions. The next priority would be View Videos and, finally, Launch Advanced Helper, which would be handled by people following the early deliveries of the solution. IT developers can then focus their efforts on what's important for the business and not what they think is the most inter-

---

[5] This saves doubled effort across projects.

esting work to do, for example, the advanced helper. Use cases provide well-defined sets of external functionality that aid IT developers in estimating the effort required. Any use-case-based delivery schedule is more realistic than the traditional approach of monolithic plans that imply "we'll be finished in two and a half years from now, at 3:30 on a Tuesday morning. . . ."

Meeting the Devil

By and large, a use-case structure is easily understood: the "devil is in the detail." Each ellipse in the diagram must have a description that outlines the course of events within the use case.

This might be complemented by more interesting details such as preconditions and postconditions.[6] If we apply a methodology or a process to our project, then a predefined document template might already be supplied. If we don't, an enterprise template is easily developed from books. In a compact approach, things that might be found in separate e-documents can be made footnotes of a use-case description instead – say, some nonfunctional requirements.

Here's a generic template as a starter for your projects:

Use Case: Request Support

Objective/business value: Minimize customer downtime by online support using semi-natural language queries for all customers

Delivery priority: High

Precondition: Customer identified and not on the hot list

Postcondition: Journal details of customer and case recorded

Steps

Actor: Enters license number

System: USE Confirm Product to match and confirm product type, and then display Fault Report form

A: Enters fault description

S: Performs case-based search and displays list of possible conditions

A: Selects closest match or requests the Advanced Helper

---

[6] Preconditions must be satisfied before the use case starts. Postconditions must be satisfied when the use case has completed.

S: USE Browse Repair Descriptions and View Videos for chosen match

A: Ends request

S: Record journal entry in case base (with customer and case details)

Footnotes

Advanced Helper is an agent-driven intelligent search (a separate future use case)

Nonfunctional requirements and constraints

As per system availability, that is, 365×24 hour, downtime < 1 hour per year

Case-based results on web server: 80 percent hit ratio (from case bases of 200,000 accumulated cases and onward).

A simple use case and yet quite a list, isn't it? Now suppose we didn't structure this as a diagram of several use cases. This initial list would double at least, overloading the mainstream by additional detail about rare courses of events.

The previous Actor-System-template is an effective reminder about the system boundary, preventing us from rushing too far from it (see the following warnings) as each A: simply "sets the agenda" here by referring to the key actor (A-Actor) in the corresponding use-case diagram.[7] This template also copes well with changing requirements, as well as with sharing use cases across projects.

The footnotes and nonfunctional requirements also provide a memory boost later. This example list indicates already that the interactions described by the use cases capture the *starting point,* rather than the full size of the project. Getting the case base and the search mechanisms in place will take effort. In other words, hard work is ahead, despite quite a simple use-case dialogue. This is often perceived as an *iceberg effect* when an enterprise connects to the web – meaning, of course, *real* sales, not simply a traditional shop window or e-brochure with a few hyperlinks. As we move the logic into the new system, many user interactions disappear, while the inside of the system gets surprisingly complex.

---

[7] Sometimes, other actors are in the use case, in which case you might choose to enlarge this A stick figure to show the A-actor is the one who triggers the use case. A similar technique is showing this is an open-headed arrow pointing from the stick figure. Although this arrow is common, some people still find it confusing because, in most A-actor cases, the flow of information is bidirectional here: both to and from the actor.

If something like a semi-manual support procedure existed before, the old system could be simple because logic looks deceptively simple, when unstructured and/or inconsistent – in human brains and Post-it notes. However, business logic in heads of clerks would, for instance, hardly provide a 365×24 service to 500 parallel users in several languages.

Use-Case Analysis at Two Levels, At Least

In both the Unified Process and Select Perspective, a clear distinction exists between a standard use case (called *system use case*) and a business use case. In *any* process or methodology (including lightweight ones), two separate steps are advisable, keeping these two levels of detail apart. To prevent endless discussions on clicks and technology issues, you can simply let the initial stage capture business events only (events like request support) and add the complete bullet list (see the previous template) in the next stage where system use cases mirror detailed user interaction, such as fill in, display, or confirm.[8]

In the beginning of a use case, the key step of defining its *business value* (or objective) hopefully implies an amount ending with many zeroes. Why bother about that? Well, adding some measurable value is the purpose of any use case. If you rush directly into detailed dialogue lists, you might miss smarter ways to the goal, such as automation instead of interaction, in the current version or in a later one. The tradeoff between user *interaction* "as usual" and *automation* is a key point we stress throughout this book. In practice, this translates into a tradeoff between use cases on the one hand, and business process and structure on the other.

An everyday-life example is paying your household bills. The objective is simply staying creditworthy/sound and free from debts. Many people find an Internet-bank dialogue state of the art. In many banks, however, there's also the automatic bill-payment option. Just pre-register all the accounts to be paid to regularly and keep receiving the household bills as usual, except for an important footnote on them, which says, provided no objection from the household (as to amount, and so forth) the money will be *transferred automatically* on date due without a human in the loop, management by exception style. All you need do is file the bills and check the quarterly reports from the account as usual. Computers simply do the daily work and humans do the auditing. The goal remains the same. The way to get there

---

[8] The initial stage includes only events corresponding to the last *confirm* (or submit-click) of each dialogue or, more precisely, the instant when a *business event* proceeds from the interface into the kernel of the system. Thus, the second stage adds the remaining "preparatory" fill-ins and clicks preceding this final confirm.

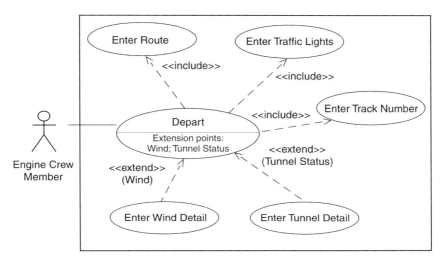

Figure 3-3a. **Interaction, MS Windows style.**

has been straightened, changing most of the complexity from external to internal (thus, no longer visible in the system use case Pay household bills).

A similar example is an engine driver on a high-velocity train. The goal is clear because the business value of the Depart use case is the quick, safe, environmentally sound transport of customers to their destination. In this case, you can either rush into dialogues and a flood of windows regarding weather, tunnel data, train priority, and so forth (as in Figure 3-3a), or you can have the driver push a Notify ATC system button and depart (as in Figure 3-3b). The dialogue is close to zero, yet, the value is added anyway.

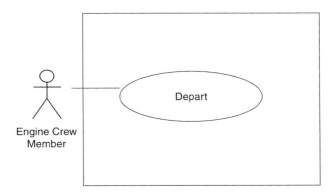

Figure 3-3b. **Automation, twenty-first-century style.** Click and let the system do the rest.

Guiding the train to its destination, today's Automatic Train Control (ATC) systems then communicate directly with the onboard software of the engine and with other engines and systems as well. Again, the goal and the value remain the same. The way to get there has been straightened, changing most of the complexity from external to internal (thus, no longer visible in the system use case Depart).

Recently, user interactions were considered by many as the essence of computing. The automation approach usually puts that view in question. The difference between the (a) and the (b) version is even bigger than the diagrams indicate. In fact, the rather interactive, use case-based version (a) of the Depart use case still omits the usual flood of technical, non-business interactions, such as restarting Windows, running Scandisk, or starting an antivirus scan – all of those too familiar to PC end users. In addition to this, the rather automated version (b) of the Depart use case also contains an extremely shrunken bullet list in its use-case description, along the lines of:

Steps

>   **Actor:** Pushes ATC button.

>   **System:** Performs the rest of the trip.

Nonfunctional requirements and constraints

>   System availability: i.e., 365×24 hour, downtime < 1 hour per year

>   System safety strategy: whenever the kernel of the system and the safety-checker subsystem arrive at different results, the system must turn the red light on and activate all brakes of the train immediately.

In fact, this rather minimal version captures the rationale behind modern ATC systems. Unsurprisingly, we've no use of the use cases from 1995 in the new, automated version as these two versions are totally different. Interestingly, however, the objective/business value of the Depart use case is exactly the same in both versions. So, although questioned by some people, the business value statement is the only part of the use-case definition likely to survive automation.

Some readers might remember a CEO of British Airways claiming that tomorrow's airplanes will be flown by a human and a dog: the human to feed the dog, the dog to bite the human in case he/she tries to touch something. Apparently, such future systems will face the delicate problem of switching the red light on and activating the brakes at the altitude of Mt. Everest or higher. A safety mechanism useful in vital air traffic software is based on triple subsystems: whenever any difference occurs in the results, two "votes" override one "vote" when the system decides on appropriate actions to be taken.

How to Avoid Messing Up Use Cases

People who are confident with use cases enjoy them, saving a lot of time and misunderstandings. Some might have difficulty getting started with this semi-formalized exercise, however, so we provide a list of traps below. Some common blind alleys constitute a risk during the early days of the project, where effort is spent on activities that have no part of the use-case approach. Converts from older methodologies often insist on trying these "mis-use cases" out in a project, but we always argue that staying away from them is cheaper because a compact and effective UML documentation is an act of balance among several views ("drawings") within a model.

The Apollo 13 Syndrome

This is all about masquerading some high-level software components as use cases, despite external interaction being equal to zero. Roughly, this is an extreme form of functional decomposition, using a hierarchy of ellipses instead of 1970-style rectangles[9] (see Figure 3-4). This is an outdated idea because functions are volatile – a typical change to a system is about altering its functionality – whereas objects and classes (see Chapter 4) provide a more stable foundation. This is why a use-case model of detailed system internals is likely to make maintenance costs skyrocket. Let classes and components provide the desired several levels of detail instead, *working outside in* (not the opposite). Maintainable use cases stay on the *system boundary,* and IT staff will later model the inside in a more formal way (for example, search scenarios) in other UML views.

The Tying-It-Here Trap

A common symptom of this is a lengthy precondition/postcondition list in each use case. Preconditions are great, if they don't cross-connect separate use cases (in other words, avoid sequencing conditions here). The more self-

---

[9] In those good ol' days, the top rectangle of a hierarchy could say "Fly to the moon" and a leaf rectangle 20 levels below could say something like "Add one to count."

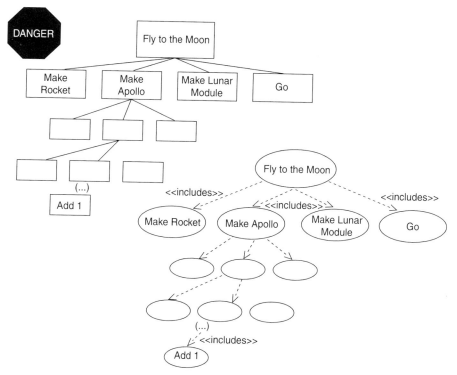

Figure 3-4. Masquerading 1970-style functional decomposition as use cases.
This (outdated) path of reasoning most often results in skyrocketing maintenance later, no
matter what the shapes. It resembles speaking the words of a new language while insisting
on grammar and phrases from one's "old" language.

contained the use cases are, the easier to change or reconfigure the business
process in the future or to share a use-case model across projects in an enterprise. This is a major point because of process redesign repeatedly altering
the process flows during a lifetime of a system.

Such sequencing conditions – not to mention manual business activities
– tend to press the entire business process into the use-case *text* template,
instead of a workflow providing literally the big *picture*, shown as an activity
diagram, across several use cases, interleaved with manual activities, if any.

Furthermore, only roles directly involved with our system-to-be become
actors, whereas those involved indirectly, say, a customer talking, faxing, or
mailing a customer agent (the real actor), are visible in the workflow or the
business use case *only*. The use-case model stays on the system boundary and
we work outside in, not from outside further outward, as in Figure 3-5.

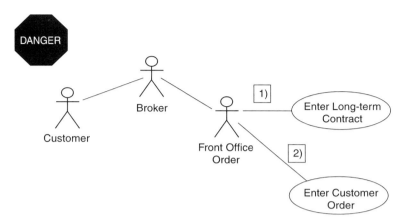

Figure 3-5. **Masquerading workflow as use cases.** This (wrong) path of reasoning makes the system too sensitive to business process redesign. It interleaves the dialogue issues into the current business process, which is likely to change in the future.

The Two-Models-in-One Trap

Many people do only a trivial use-case model, and then draw separate activity diagrams for each use case. With a tricky dialogue flow, consisting of loops and conditional steps, this might become necessary, but there's some risk of structure moving away from *one* use-case diagram structure into *many* activity diagrams. Generally speaking, use-case diagrams are powerful in mirroring interaction structure and in keeping the interactions easy to reconfigure as the business changes, while activity diagrams are powerful in showing the big picture across several use cases in a business process flow, or the workflow view. In a well-balanced UML model, changes in a business process affect the activity diagram and *not* the rest.

The Value-Is-Self-Evident Trap

Rushing past use-case objective and business value right into interactions is a 1990s PC-style approach. We find modern automation approaches more often in IBM's system management tools or in EHP Telecom's[10] telecom network management tools than in enterprise systems. On the other side of the PC coin, some under-automation occurred because of a preoccupation with simple office software packages and the person in the loop. This leaves end users with an information overload (too much to see), and powerful servers lying increasingly idle. Often, e-business provided the lesson here, triggering

---

[10] Originally founded by Ericsson and Hewlett-Packard.

a renewed focus on automation of the business processes, for example, try visiting web sites for home insurance[11] quotes and see how automated these processes have become.

As mentioned, an explicit *business value* statement in a use case even provides valuable hints on shortcuts and on how to eliminate the entire use case in a future version of our system – by automation, by simplified business processes, or by both.

The Smart Response Trap

This is when use cases tell too little about the system with an advanced *kernel* hidden behind trivial interactions (Actor: Enters Query. Expert system: displays advice . . .). Other UML diagrams are used to capture important aspects of a knowledge base or of complex batch and agent systems. Often, we also need two rather simple use cases because of a time gap, splitting two business events apart. For instance, number 1 "Order a batch report" done by a human actor during office hours and number 2 "Run all the batch jobs," which is triggered at night by a separate actor, such as a Scheduler system.

Similarly, a Data warehouse or MIS might process aggregated data in 20 dimensions and display the results on the Web, GPRS/3G, Windows (all ten versions of them) as tables, waves, bars, cheeses, and so forth. This might make the layouts differ, but as long as the course of events in the user interaction is the same, we're well off with only *one* use case covering all those alternatives (see the box on the opposite page).

The Use-Class Trap

Many classes in an enterprise system correspond to business entities, typically persisting a series of use cases, with long idle periods between the use cases. For example, a customer order goes through various stages in the business process that alter the order's state, say, from confirmed, to picked, to en route, to delivered, to paid, along the lines of Figure 3-6. Some people tend to merge several use cases regarding the same entity, but this is wrong. The boundaries between use cases are provided by *timing*, not by components or classes affected inside the system. Later, a state diagram showing the entity life cycle tells the desired "dynamic" story per class, for example, for the Customer-order class in our example.

Thus, use cases triggered on the *same* occasion are usually related, whereas use cases affecting the same entity at different points in time aren't related. Keeping the use-case view *apart* from the internal views (see the fol-

---

[11] Examples are *www.theAA.com, www.insurancecenter.com.*

PARAMETERIZED USE CASES

At the moment, neither UML nor the tools support *parameterized* use cases. By adding such a compact construct, you can visualize the same dialogue being performed with *different input values* resulting in *different output layouts* (or sorting, and so forth), yet leaving the course of events unchanged. This saves dozens of trivial (and wrong) extends or generalizations between use cases, especially in MIS, Data Warehousing, or knowledge applications. Until having future standards and tools at hand, an enterprise can create some temporary enterprise-wide agreement, for example, using color or some proprietary UML-stereotype on the use-case icon («parameterized») or, tools permitting, a UML dashed square listing the parameters on top of the use-case icon,* as shown in Figure B3-3.

For example, imagine a weekly report per country and city, sorted alphabetically from *A* to *Z* and showing market-share data as yellow "cheeses" on a map. This certainly differs in form and content from a quarterly report per product family and product, sorted in descending order by launch-date and showing net margin as amber-colored top portions of black bars of turnover. Some people tend to view this variance (in layouts) as several use cases, arriving at wallpaper-sized use-case models. To prevent a

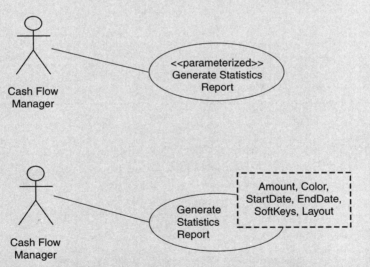

Figure B3-3. Parameterizing a use case for varying outputs – an example of enterprise customization of a standard UML construct. Very different candy is going to come out of the machinery, yet through the same course of events (dialogue steps) – in other words, through the same use case.

---

* The example reflects the fact that this compact approach typically fits systems or components that provide information to decision-makers, atop the "operations information" provided to doers in everyday business.

(continued)

PARAMETERIZED USE CASES *(cont.)*

conflict within the project between this wallpaper view and the compact view, we simply use parameters to indicate differences will exist (between the kinds of "candy" being output), yet sticking to only *one* use case (Figure B3-3), as long as the course of events in the dialogue is the same.

Notably, in both these examples, even the look of the user interface can be made the same for both print requests: the actor selects kinds of amounts to be printed, output colors, sort keys, and so forth by clicking on sliders and list boxes on the same screen, no matter what the exact combination of output being requested.**An individual user might save a completely filled-in "favorite screen" or three for frequent print requests (to reuse the filled-in values repeatedly, by simply clicking a Print button). But to the system, all these are only *one* kind of layout with different input values. Thus, both the dynamics of the dialogues (the use case) and the static look of the user interfaces remain the *same*. The mapping from different input values to their corresponding output variants can be performed[†] by components in the kernel of the system.

** *Stereotypes* are UML's amending mechanism to be used in creating your own variants of a standard UML construct, which is what we're doing with UML use cases here. The *dashed square* is a standard way of depicting parameterization in UML class diagrams (the structural view explained in Chapter 4).

[†] Like parameterization in general, this technique not only makes the documentation compact, it also greatly simplifies upgrades of the system. For example, producing a new combination of output on a report in the future affects neither the course of the dialogue nor the layout of the user interface. On these two reasons, a similar parameterized approach comes in handy even later, at the technical design level, for example, in making only one user interface of only one system fit many countries, languages, amount formats, date formats, and so forth.

---

lowing chapters) makes things easier, preventing a split of focus.[12] Also, if you build application software, rather than an access control utility, actors from the use-case view needn't correspond to classes in the structural view either.

The Useless User Trap

On one hand, end users of our system-to-be are a useful speaking partner in human-computer interaction issues (dialogues, layouts, and so forth). On the other hand, they're often useless in big picture issues like business process redesign, simplified work flow, business use cases, or an enterprise business rule. They can, however, provide valuable hints on current practices breaking that business rule. Many projects run into a communication

---

[12] Later, when we model the internal dynamics of the use-case interactions, UML sequence diagrams tie the classes (via their objects) to the relevant use cases.

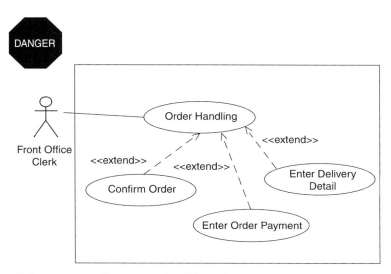

Figure 3-6. Masquerading an entity life cycle as use case extends (a menu-design-zealot view). This path of reasoning makes business events difficult to track in the model. Use cases can be interrelated if they happen at the same time, whereas, in this example, they are triggered by *separate business events* on separate occasions. Therefore, all three of them must be separate use cases related directly to the actor. How each of them affects the order can be shown in a state diagram (see Chapter 5).

nightmare, which is easily avoided by simply having *the right roles decide on the right issues*.

The Traditional Waterfall Project Trap

If you think the use-case model is 100 percent finished, then something is wrong. It might be good – meaning easily modified, modular, well structured, self-contained – rather than finished forever. Requirement specifications and use cases in particular, do change at the same pace as business and the forecasted rate of change is bad news for the traditional "waterfall" approach to software projects. However, shared effort applies also to changes in requirements. Changes within the use-case model have to be clarified, estimated, priced, and planned by business and IT in cooperation.

Whatever the step, remember, all modern methodologies are explicitly *iterative*. Therefore, use-case analysis reaches its peak early in the project, but it doesn't block parallel work on other UML diagrams. The particular mix of issues and diagrams on our agenda depends on the nature of our particular proposed system (see Chapter 4 for the structural view).

Summary

Now that we've defined the requirements with use cases, we're ready to specify the internals of the system in the next chapters – with classes, components, and their interactions with each other to deliver the functionality shown in use cases.

- Use cases define the *system boundary,* which is where we keep the use-case modeling effort, too. We avoid a skid into internal detail, as well as a skid into the surrounding business, away from the proposed system.

- Use cases define system activities in terms of *external functionality* based on business events.

- Use cases are powerful with systems that are going to *interact* extensively with end users or other systems, whereas with many MIS, Data Warehouse, or knowledge systems, we're happy with few (possibly parameterized) use cases.

- Use cases involve *actors* that might be people or other systems. Actors are the *source* where use cases come from and, thus, are a good starting point.

- Use-case diagrams provide the *structure of the interactions* between the actors and the system. Also, each use case must be complemented by a structured *bullet list.*

- Use cases aid *most stakeholders* from analysis and design to project planning and management.

Chapter 4
Sketching the
Inside Structure

*N**ow that we've specified** the external requirements, we begin mapping our system-to-be by sketching out its internal structure, gradually involving more IT personnel. Involvement of the stakeholders depends on the nature of the system. If the system is to be highly interactive, then much of the hard work has already been done during specifying and defining the use cases. If the system-to-be is more complex than interactive, such as a knowledge base, then you might have to do much more work at this stage, for example, detailing the rules that affect each part of the solution.

We're also dependent on the skills of our IT personnel. Throughout the project, experienced people familiar with both object methodology and conceptual thinking will ask many of the important questions early in the specification stage, whereas new converts will appreciate more input from other stakeholders, including help with first-cut key diagrams.

Because structure issues are key with most enterprise systems, we provide boxes on some advanced constructs, as well as extensive footnotes on details and semi-technical issues. We point out why some peripheral, or seemingly peripheral, questions often emerge during modeling.

Some methodologies encourage a two-step process on defining classes: first, model the business classes (the first cut), and then develop a complete class model. In a lightweight approach, we can view these as two levels of detail, which then gives an indication of the involvement of relevant business expertise. The purpose of first-cut business class diagrams is to boost communication between stakeholders and IT personnel on issues uncovered during any development project. We use these class diagrams as a *map of the domain,* showing the key elements (the kernel) of the system, as well as validating and verifying our use cases and process flow. This feedback loop is a crucial part of the development process. By using the small set of UML diagrams, we can be sure, at each stage, the previous work still holds true. If not, then we can change it early, thus avoiding later problems at the coding and testing stages.

Class diagrams are crucial throughout the whole development cycle. As we move forward, IT people add considerable technical detail to the kernel, including the technical components. Many of those, like user interface components of forms and buttons, are easily read "between the lines" of a use case and its layout examples, while some require more experience.[1] Along with this, IT people are also responsible for making the structure maintainable and making its components reusable. Getting it simple and general is vital, but this takes skills and time, as with most hi-tech products.

Class Diagrams

The structural foundation of our system-to-be is modeled in standard UML class diagrams. As mentioned in the previous chapter, use cases capture functional and, thus, volatile requirements, changing in future versions of our system. *Class diagrams,* on the other hand, provide a static model in the positive sense of the word. First, class diagrams model *structure,* which is a static view, while other UML views provide the dynamic aspects. Second, in the business logic layer (the kernel of our system-to-be), class diagrams mirror real-world business artifacts, which undergo notably less change than the functional requirements or the workflows. For example, from our initial system for a few medieval-style pubs and all the way to our Wet-Liquids.com net version (year 2080 style, extended functionality), the kernel of the system would consist of rather timeless classes like Customer, Serving (or Portion), Drink (or Beverage), Invoice, and so forth. Thus, class diagrams set the stage, resilient to changing scenarios. This is sometimes called *isomor-*

---

[1] All the detail is because of later automation: UML tools provide ("generate") the structure-dependent parts of the code, in our particular programming language, instead of spending weeks writing those parts manually.

phism: the real-world objects from the real-world business are mirrored in their original form, directly in the system.

Strengths

Class diagrams are powerful on structural aspects. Much of their power is because of modularity: although quite self-contained, many classes simply complement each other. In practice, 80 percent of our classes might be the "same as except . . . ," that is, the same as some existing class except for a few additional details – as is the case with Beverage and SoftDrink, as shown in Figure 4-1. UML provides a construct called *generalization,* that enables you to build layers of hierarchy from the generic down to the specific. For example, we all have different kinds of bank accounts: checking account, savings account, credit card account, loan account, stock account, and so forth which have common features—account number, account holder, date opened, various operations such as doWithdrawal or doDeposit, and so forth – that can now be defined *once* in a class called Bank Account. If you didn't do this generalization, then you would be facing the burden of alter-

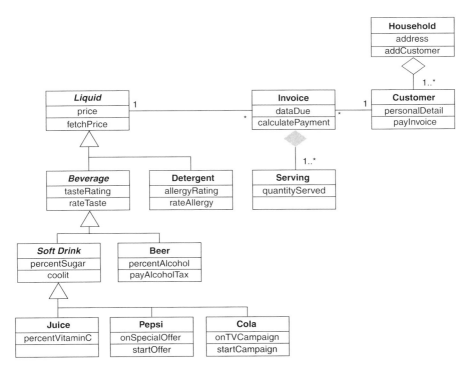

Figure 4-1. **The timeless aspect.** An example class diagram for Wet-Liquids.com.

ing, on every upgrade, these common features in every kind of bank account again and again.

Limitations
Life cycles, messages such as transaction steps or signals passed between objects within the system (see Chapter 5) and external functionality/use cases (see Chapter 3), all belong to other UML diagrams.

The Class Diagram

Each class in the diagram starts as a simple box icon with a name to which features (attributes and operations) are added. Later, the final class definition will include a complete list of all its features. In a first-cut class diagram, we might prefer to show a key operation (or three) that handles key business events. For example, in Figure 4-1, there is no class called "Payment," which implies a payment-processing operation is probably a part of Invoice.[2] As we discover first-cut business classes, we track the purpose of each class.[3] For the example of Invoice, we can say it has to record sold items, to calculate monies due, to record payments, and to issue receipts. We can then leave the precise class definition to the IT personnel.

Getting There
There are two families of *class-discovery* strategies:

- *Business semantics*-driven, which focuses on attributes (data).

- *Business service*-driven, which focuses on business events to be processed (behavior), as understood from use cases and the dynamic UML views.

In practice, we recommend a mix. If your project colleagues are experienced in data modeling, then stress business events to start. If the majority of your colleagues are experienced programmers, though, then stress (initially) business semantics (data) instead. This initial push is to ensure a *long-term balance* in the mix of strategies, roughly fifty-fifty.

In our thirst-slaking business of Wet-Liquids.com, we begin by discovering the key business concepts (usually identified as the nouns in documents,

---

[2] We read such important operations almost as a part of the *structure*. This operation tells indirectly why the Payment class wasn't considered necessary.

[3] In some cases, the enterprise might predefine its own, rather extended, set of class stereotypes. Where this isn't the case, we can use other means of expressing the purpose of a class, for example, by listing high-level, business-event-related operations of that class.

OCL AND KNOWLEDGE TOOLS
TRY TO RULE OUT RULE TROUBLES

With complex business rules, the UML's Object Constraint Language (OCL) is powerful, but still rarely understood by many software specialists unfamiliar with combining declarative business rules with a class structure. At the same time, lawyers and controllers of today are unfamiliar with classes and how class relationships can keep the business rules where they're applicable – instead of causing a flood of exceptions to general rules, which, in turn, complicate enterprise systems even further.

Knowledge tools, on the other hand, do provide support for complex business rules (for example, in telecom management or in finance). This kind of support enables seniors or process owners to enter the rules into the system directly without traditional programming, IT specialists then advise on tests, structure, maintainability, reuse, and so forth. At the moment, full UML and OCL are often only a "future feature" in a knowledge tool. Wherever the tool offers some industry-specific graphical "language" that models the business logic, however, this is the easiest way to go (for example, in telecom network management or financial analyses).

including our use-case descriptions), as well as the key business events. Skilled IT people can provide other stakeholders with a checklist as a starting point and with a process framework or a book chapter as a guideline. Initially, we might arrive at a few dozen classes, whereas in a final, detailed version for a full-scale object ERP package, IT staff might arrive at several hundred (or even a few thousand) classes later. Some of these classes are essential and will be encountered early. We then work through the structure *middle out* – from business to technical, from key to peripheral, from typical up to more general or down to more special.[4]

Although denoted by a noun in the *singular*, a class always defines *all* objects of the same kind.[5] For example, Customer would define *all* individual customers, that is, the *common* features of all of them. Serving defines *all* individual servings, and so on.

---

[4] You might even face an initial explosion of candidate classes in the first iterations if you tend to document every key concept as a class. However, this will get better soon! Techniques are down the road (parameterization, extensive use of associations, and many others) to make the structure simpler and easier to maintain. Classes have to be grouped into high-level components (packages) simplifying reuse and maintenance. IT staff assist other stakeholders in keeping the model robust and tidy.

[5] The *italicized* (or abstract) classes like *Beverage* don't supply any objects themselves. Instead, they simply come in handy as superclasses of other classes, which, in turn, supply the individual objects. For example, Pepsi supplies Pepsi objects. Again, this becomes important later, rather than at this initial conceptual stage, so simply accept some italicized UML-class names as something the IT people will need soon.

CLASSES AND OBJECTS

A clear distinction exists between a *class* and an individual *instance* of that class. This instance is called an object. We discover, design, and write/generate code for the classes; these are static in nature. *Objects* run (inside the computer) as instances of a class; these are dynamic in nature. For any class, many objects might be running (inside the computer) at any one time and each can be referenced by a unique identifier value, for example, "portfolio_number_77". Throughout the project, a class diagram documents the proposed structure of the system, whereas an object diagram can illustrate some individual example objects in the system if requsted by some stakeholder.

A significant and twofold difference occurs between a class diagram and the more traditional data models you might have seen before. First, you use several *kinds* of standard *relationships* (see the following). Second, each class icon has three main parts: its name, its attributes, and its operations that work on the attributes. For example, class Invoice not only has attributes, such as dateDue, it also has operations. The most important operation is probably calculatePayment.[6]

Understanding Class Relationships

Four types of relationships occur between classes:

- **Association:** a very loose relationship, which might even be rather short term and changing. Similar to one between a company and the rental cars currently hired by that company.

- **Aggregation:** whole-part, a "medium," typically long-term relationship. By and large, similar to a long-term cooperation of your firm with your A customers (frame agreement, minority ownership, and so forth).

- **Composition:** whole-part, a strictly defined lifetime relationship. Similar to one between your office building and its floors.

- **Generalization:** general-specific, a structural relationship. Similar

---

[6] To challenge the old axioms given by many developers with a data modeling background, we chose this operation in Invoice, instead of having a Payment class. This would be considered rare in a data model because operations aren't visible there. However, in the opposite case, if this book were intended to make programmers switch to conceptual thinking, we would probably challenge *their* old axioms by stressing the attributes instead.

to the kinship between savings account and account in general (of all kinds).

These all can be combined on any class diagram, so it's important you understand their characteristics. The distinctions between them are quite important as they're interpreted the same way throughout: by stakeholders, by designers/software developers, as well as by software tools.[7]

Associations

The most common relationship is an *association,* which is shown as a straight line linking classes in the diagram (this is similar to the "traditional" data modeling association). During the modeling exercise, the following keywords indicate an association:

- connected
- associated to
- related

So we're not too specific about the relationship.[8]

We're interested in the minimum and maximum number (of instances) being related between the classes. This is called *cardinality* or *multiplicity,* meaning the possible range of numbers on each side of the association. This has been extremely non-standardized in the past. Fortunately, UML defines the symbols to be used at each end of the associations. Examples are * (the same as the more explicit 0..*), which means zero, one, or more; 0..1, which means an optional one; and 1..*, which means one or more. These are "read" from the opposite side of the association, for example, one customer per invoice and multiple invoices per customer. *One liquid per serving* means we don't mix different liquid sales on one serving – which would result in a rather long setup time on our liquid-package switching hardware, version

---

[7] Such as code generators, object database engines, or (likely) future database technology standards, such as ANSI SQL3.

[8] Association names, as well as association-role names, simply illustrate the purpose of the association – the relationship still staying as *loose* as an unlabeled one. When more than one association is between the same two, we *name* each of the association links or the roles on either side. For example, a Customer might be associated to several telephone lines (with role names such as home, mobile, home office, and so forth). Then, a billing system can easily specify those phone lines as three entries on a bill (called home, mobile, and home office), in addition to a bottom line stating "your total bill this month."

2080. If we did intermix in that way, we'd have to show this as a many-to-many association instead between Liquid and Invoice (* at both ends).

The association between Liquid and Invoice relates it to any kind of liquid, whether a detergent or any beverage, that is, invoices don't care whether liquids rinse throats or baths.[9]

Aggregation

A whole-part relationship is called an *aggregation* (shown as a diamond and a line between two classes in Figure 4-2). Classes in an aggregation aren't only connected, they constitute a "whole" from a business perspective. For example, a household site consists of one or more customers; an e-trader customer might consist of one or more portfolios.

Example keywords indicating an aggregation:

- has a . . .

- consists of, are parts of (respectively)

- whole and part/s

So we're rather specific about the *kind* of the relationship.

The normal number at the diamond side, that is, at the "whole" of an aggregation, is exactly 1 and, therefore, it can be implied where it isn't explicitly stated, as is the case in the diagram. In an association, it would be read as undefined, instead of implied because there's no concept of a part or a whole in an association. The whole is what makes it possible to imply the 1 in aggregations (Figure 4-2). In your first UML project or three, however, being overly explicit is a good idea, always showing the 1 (even in aggregations[10]). Remember, the point of UML is reducing ambiguity. Here, we have to figure out what exactly our project colleagues call unambiguous.

The zero in 0..* is useful down the road because a common cause of error is wrong program code in a program loop processing a "collection" of objects that happens to be empty (zero objects) in the particular case. By showing the zero explicitly, we remind the system developer upfront of this

---

[9] The relationship between these two is rather loose. Invoices assume liquids to rinse *in whatever way* and to do whatever else is the purpose of the Liquid class – invoices just minding their own "money business."

[10] Unlike in a composition relationship, a part of an aggregation can (rarely, but still) belong to several "wholes" at the same time. For example, a parking lot belonging to two office buildings or a driveway belonging to two houses. Both examples are long-term relationships, but to two wholes. So, while composition parts always belong to "mandatory one" whole, aggregation parts belong to typically one whole. Therefore, implying the 1 makes sense, even in an aggregation where no number was explicitly stated.

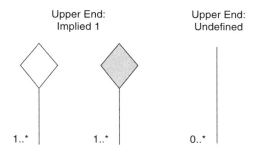

Figure 4-2. **Implied 1 in aggregation and composition.**

risk. This very simple example shows that unambiguous "blueprints" of the system improve quality, lead time, and cost levels.

Composition
UML also provides a stronger, restricted degree of aggregation called *composition* and marked by a solid, filled-in diamond on the whole side (see Figure 4-2). Composition would tell we're sure every part belongs throughout its *lifetime* to exactly one whole and removing a whole always has the effect of removing all the parts as well.[11]

The key question to ask of any aggregation is "are the lifetimes the same?" If they are, then it's a composition and, otherwise, it's a simple aggregation.

In Figure 4-1, the relationship between the Invoice and the Serving is a composition because when the Invoice is deleted, we're no longer interested in the Servings. Also, we don't move individual servings across invoices. In contrast, we have a simple aggregation between the Household and Customer because they might have different lifespans as our online customers grow up from their teens, starting new household sites, but still keeping their original customer number, gold customer status, and so forth. So, changes on either side of the aggregation relationship are neither very frequent nor banned.

You can view the empty diamonded aggregation as a gray zone kind of relationship between association and composition. Selecting from these three when drawing a particular first-cut class diagram brings about some modeling difficulty to people unfamiliar with UML (later on during design,

---

[11] When deleting an object , that object first tells the object on the other side of the relationship "I'm disappearing," that is, any link between them will no longer work. In a composition relationship, deleting the whole then cascades to deleting all the parts as well. In a multitier architecture, such consistency issues can be automated by a separate handler class, monitoring each relationship and even synchronizing the tiers of the system. This technology keeps technical operations apart from business classes.

however, this distinction isn't a big technical issue). Therefore, we develop a common example a bit further here, as shown in Figure 4-3.

Trains are a frequently used example of aggregation. They consist of an engine and one or more railroad cars, but the degree or strength of the relationship varies, depending on the proposed system's view of the domain. In a train project, we would probably start from the empty aggregation diamond, and then raise additional questions as we move on. For most trains, the aggregation relationship holds true: a whole exists, the relationship is not extremely short term and, yet, it isn't a lifetime one.

For some other train company, composition might provide the correct picture. Suppose the owner of the future system is an operator of high-velocity trains, with a strict safety policy of always checking the entire train, even if only a minor failure occurs on one of the cars. In such a case, we ask the questions about lifetimes early. Suppose the company has a policy of always buying only a *complete* train at a time, as well as scraping (or disposing of, in some way) only a complete train all at once. This makes the *lifetime* of the cars equal to the lifetime of the train. For such trains (where we're certain of this), the composition relationship holds true: a whole does exist and the relationship is a lifetime one.

For yet another train company system, association might provide the correct picture. Suppose we're specifying a freight-car ledger system intended to be used by many train operators from several countries, pooling their cars across an entire continent. Here, we probably ask several additional questions early to take a closer look at the whole. The business specialists might tell us about cars being switched frequently from one train to another. Maybe they tell us real-life stories about cars spending months just standing

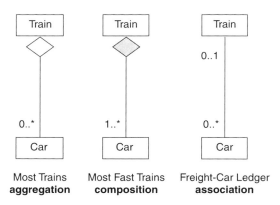

Figure 4-3. **Medium, close, and loose relationships.** The coupling between trains and railroad cars varies, depending on the proposed system's view of the domain.

GENERALIZATIONS IN ADVANCED MODELING

In the UML, we can even tackle less-frequent cases, where the generalization structure is more than only one straightforward hierarchy. Such cases bring about technical difficulty, rather than modeling difficulty.* In fact, the first-cut class diagrams are made quite compact by these techniques, saying each detail only once. In practice, these cases are encountered less often, so both modeling techniques shown here are advanced/powerful, rather than commonplace.

In some systems with a sophisticated logic, typically where the system-to-be is able to use several views or paths of reasoning, several generalization fork arrows can point to the same superclass. For example, along with the classification in our previous class diagram, liquids can be classified as domestic, NAFTA, or overseas, in which case, all we've said about Liquid applies to all its subclasses in *both* generalization structures under Liquid. This is called *multiple classification*. We label each of the generalizations by a discriminator, for example, Region of Origin, as shown in Figure B4-1.

In some systems with an extensive reuse of classes, several generalization arrows

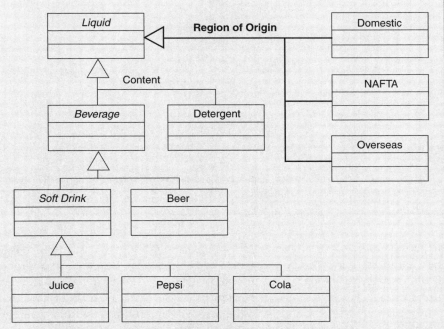

Figure B4-1. Multiple classification from Liquid can combine customer value and custom value in Wet-Liquid.com's logistics.

---

* The limitations of commonplace programming languages can be circumnavigated by standard solutions, such as a design pattern.

(continued)

GENERALIZATIONS IN ADVANCED MODELING *(cont.)*

can point from the same subclass. For example, some people might argue that they classify Cola as *both* beverage *and* detergent because of its effect on stain spots. If this is so, then all we've said about Beverage and Detergent also applies to Cola, as in Figure B4-2. This is called *multiple inheritance.*

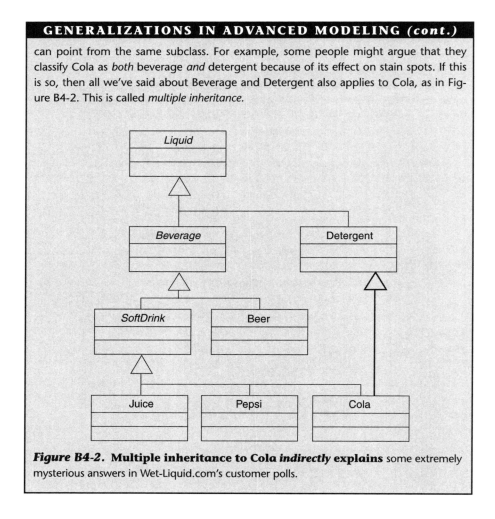

***Figure B4-2.* Multiple inheritance to Cola *indirectly* explains** some extremely mysterious answers in Wet-Liquid.com's customer polls.

on private sidings and dead ends "somewhere far south," and then being thoroughly serviced directly on return to their owner company. In addition to disconnecting the lifetimes, this makes the concept of a train extremely fuzzy. In fact, while standing forgotten in a dead end, a car doesn't belong to any train at all. For such trains, the association relationship holds true: no clear whole exists and the relationship to a train is usually short term.

Generalization

A general-specific relationship is called a *generalization* – shown as an arrow and a line between classes in the diagram. Example keywords indicating a generalization:

- is, is a, is always a . . .

- is the same as . . . except . . .

- is (at the same time) even a . . .

Again, we're rather specific about the *kind* of the relationship.

The generalization class structure is usually called a *class hierarchy* (or *tree*) linking superclasses and their subclasses. For example in Figure 4-1, Pepsi is a subclass of SoftDrink, which is, in turn, the superclass of Pepsi.

This is a rather close, clear-box style relationship. All we say about Soft-Drink applies automatically to Pepsi. When used in a unified, organized manner, this saves much time and makes things easier in upgrades and new versions of our system.[12]

Summary

- Class diagrams show the *structure* of the parts of the system and how they're interrelated. These diagrams are key in enterprise systems.

- Class diagrams are two level: business and detailed IT/technical.

- Among all the UML views in a requirement specification, business-level class diagram is the least changing (and exceptions to this rule of thumb aren't frequent[13]).

- When completed, each class definition icon contains class name, operations, and attributes.

- A class diagram combines four kinds of relationship: association, aggregation, composition, and generalization.

---

[12] For example, the attribute called percentSugar, in the SoftDrink class can be computed on by operations in any of its subclasses, without explicitly copying that attribute from SoftDrink. Therefore, the programmer of Pepsi, for example, needs to know all the detailed features of SoftDrink and its superclasses.

[13] For example, in a knowledge base reflecting a research-intensive domain where "truths" are frequently changed or on some (rare) mergers when trying to harmonize systems from different sectors of industry.

Chapter 5

Sketching the Inside Dynamics

Having set the stage with class diagrams, we'll now look more closely at what is likely to happen on that stage. We examine life cycles and (with the assistance of IT staff) interactions between all the small parts within the system.

State Diagrams

Some business entities have interesting life cycles because of real-world regularities and constraints, such as business rules, legislation, laws of nature, and so forth governing their "lives." Because these business entities are represented by a class, we model this dynamic aspect in a *state diagram* per class.[1]

---

[1] Many analysts might perceive UML state diagrams as an upgrade and standardization, not too far from their early experience in entity life-cycle modeling using, for example, some old variant of state diagrams or M. A. Jackson's JSD or Bo Sundgren's models of business entity careers.

In most enterprises, some *key business entities* have an interesting life cycle, which makes a state diagram necessary. These examples show the key states (life-cycle phases) for certain key entities in different industries:

- Banking: Account (in_credit – overdrawn – blocked – overdrawn and blocked – closed)

- Travel: Reservation (registered – on waiting list – reserved – paid)

- Brokerage, shares, bonds: Order (placed – activated at desired price – deal-confirmed – closed)

- Insurance: Retirement plan (employed – payment-aged – retired – deactivated)

We find such key entities in practically *any* business. The latter example simply mirrors *the* life cycle from a retirement plan point of view.

Strengths
A state diagram is a compact, yet quite intuitive, notation. These diagrams are versatile because they can mirror the lifetime dynamics of a rather long "life" in the kernel of an enterprise system, as well as a rather short "life" in a user dialogue or in a real-time system.[2] A process owner/stakeholder is primarily involved in the long life cycles because of their business nature. Basically, we're diagramming *one category of business rules,* although not all categories: the rules dependent on states and state changes. Therefore, the states of key business entities can be modeled in parallel with early class diagrams, which means stakeholder involvement is needed with both class *and* state diagrams. That will prevent force-fitting the life-cycle aspects into use cases; in order to stay easy to reconfigure, a use case usually mirrors a *single* business event in a much *longer* life cycle of an entity.

Limitations
A UML state diagram models *one class* and *all events* relevant to that class, which is confusing for some people with a technical/real-time background, where only one traditional wallpaper-sized state diagram tended to depict the entire system.[3] *Sequence diagrams* (see the following) show the complementary dynamic view, *per business event* and across *all classes* affected.

---

[2] The path of reasoning is rather similar in both models, except for the clock ticking days-to-decades in the long, persistent case, but ticking nanoseconds-to-seconds in the short, transient case. In addition, state diagrams can even show parallel behavior where necessary, using bars, as shown with business process flows in activity diagrams (see Chapter 2).

[3] Such diagrams are trying to represent the complexity of a "state-machine."

We need state diagrams for relevant classes only (for irrelevant classes, see the boxes).

Mainstream Before Detail

Again, dynamic models *start from the mainstream,* that is, the trouble-free, golden case, happy path scenarios. The mainstream version of a state diagram is worth being maintained on its own because it will easily guide us back into the basic business logic during future upgrades of our system.

If the life cycle fits all kinds of beverages (that is, not liquids in general because there's no need to proof taste detergents!), we then can create a state model for Beverage, as shown in Figure 5-1. This means these states apply to all its subclasses as well because, for example, a Cola *is* a beverage.

The boxes with rounded corners (Figure 5-1) are *states,* which *take some time.*[4] We can, therefore, use state names in continuous present (*-ing,* in English). The arrows denote business *events* that are *instantaneous* in the system,

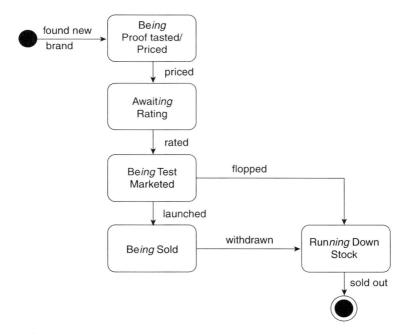

Figure 5-1. **State diagram of the Beverage class.**

---

[4] Again, whether "time" is measured in milliseconds or decades depends on the nature of the class. Key *business* entities typically have rather *long lives and slow clocks* (ticking from days up to years).

UNINTERESTING LIFE CYCLES

Boring Life Cycles

We draw state diagrams for relevant classes only. Therefore, we skip *boring life cycles,** that is, states of trivial classes with an *overrestricted* set of possible business events. For example, things in the universe get born, changed, and die, repeating the same procedure forever, so there's no point in hundreds of extremely trivial state diagrams for that in an enterprise system. Typical examples of boring life cycles are the "life" of a list of income tax percentages per household size or of a list of town names per ZIP code. These are only created, changed, and removed – a universal story, which we've heard many times before (Figure B5-1).

Unstructured Life Cycles

*Unstructured life cycles,*** that is, those of *totally unrestricted,* solely event-driven classes aren't very interesting either. Even if such a class might have something like states, they're of little importance in the model because they don't restrict the set of possible events in each state. Its behavior is virtually "stateless," permitting any business event to occur at any time. With such classes, the resulting state depends only on the *event,*

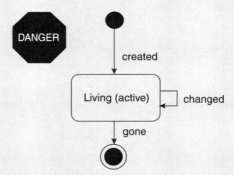

Figure B5-1. State diagram of a boring life cycle having "nothing interesting to say" in UML. This adds much clutter to the state model, thus, discouraging many people from reading it. This is unnecessary because the basic rule of nature diagrammed here is generally known and applies to any object. Avoid it.

---

* Along the lines of simplified TV-sofa psychology, some people call them neurotic life cycles, as the objects of such a class "don't dare" to engage in other business events, except these rather self-evident ones. In the early days of system development, Michael A. Jackson pioneered the term *boring structures* for this kind of non-diagrams. We find both terms quite humorous, but "boring" sounds more self-explanatory.

** To stay consistent with simplified TV-sofa psychology, this would translate to psychotic life cycles because the objects of such a class exhibit any kind of behavior at any time, no matter what their current state or the rules and logic governing commonsense behavior. Again, of these quite humorous terms, Jackson's sounds more self-explanatory (he pioneered *unstructured structures*) for this kind of pointless diagram.

(continued)

UNINTERESTING LIFE CYCLES *(cont.)*

no matter the original, preceding state. If connected to a user interface, all user options are always enabled and valid (in any state being displayed in the window). For example, none of the click buttons in that interface is ever shadowed. For this kind of class, we're happy with a simple list, instead of a state diagram:

Name of Event	*Name of Resulting State*
created	State A
a	State A
b	State B
c	State C
gone	(Nonexistent)

Note: all events can occur in all states, except the "created" event (which can only create a *new,* recently "nonexistent" object).

As we can see, the list is more compact and comprehensive than a diagram (Figure B5-2) in this particular kind of cases, which are extremely rare with key business entities. This is because it corresponds to, for example, deposits and withdrawals being

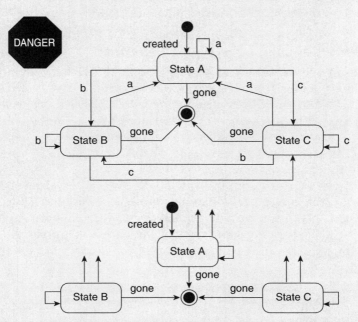

Figure B5-2. Stateless states. A state diagram of an unstructured life cycle, *"saying too much and without structure"* in UML. No matter if it's standard syntax (upper part) or compact syntax (lower part, "shorthand"), no interesting sequences or cycles exist to care about because any of the events can occur in any of the states.

(continued)

UNINTERESTING LIFE CYCLES *(cont.)*

allowed at any time, even on overdrawn or closed accounts. As shown in the list of example key business entities in this chapter, their life cycles are much more predefined and regulated in practice by a set of business rules (making state diagrams worthwhile[†]).

In our experience, the *real* danger with both boring and unstructured life cycles is in not seeing the regularities in "real" life cycles as they might seem to be one of these sorts to a less-skilled analyst at first glance (or maybe both of these sorts at the same time – to an extremely unskilled analyst). Both give us a false sensation of "modeling," without helping us at all to visualize some relevant business logic.

[†] In some code generators, however, state diagrams for classes with boring or unstructured life cycles might be used to make the code generator do what you want. Nevertheless, such tricks are for design and implementation, that is, neither requirement specification nor analysis activities.

---

rather than continuous, so we avoid the "-ing" in event names. For example, the state of a Beverage Be*ing* test-marketed can be changed by two kinds of business event: either a full-scale launch or a flop.[5]

Error Handling

State diagrams also greatly improve *error handling*. So, IT staff will most often also maintain a more complex version covering important unusual scenarios. For example, a few customers happy with Cola as a detergent might make strange cycles (of business events) happen in a consumer poll system. Or, some odd, outdated Web browser might (wrongly) permit a withdrawal request to reach a closed account in an e-bank, thus, requiring some appropriate error message from the system.

Even those scenarios are most often a worthwhile investment because, without life cycle models, error handling grows inconsistent and excessively complex as it gets 'improved' by generations of programmers. At the same time, because no one is keeping track of the normal life cycle and the big picture, the mainstream is polluted from a large number of muddy, zigzag "side streams."[6]

---

[5] Events coming into the system via an external interface, for example, by a button click, a bar code scan, or a signal from an external system. With a business entity, each event typically corresponds to the last Submit-Click in each use-case dialogue.

[6] Technical, "non-business" error handling is worth standardizing throughout the enterprise. In such cases, we diagram its principles only once, omitting them in the rest of our state diagrams. Later, during design, many errors can be blocked on input (by filter classes, apart from our business class) or prevented by techniques such as blocking all invalid click button options ahead of each dialogue step. Otherwise, error handling tends to multiply complexity, which is good to know in advance when estimating construction time.

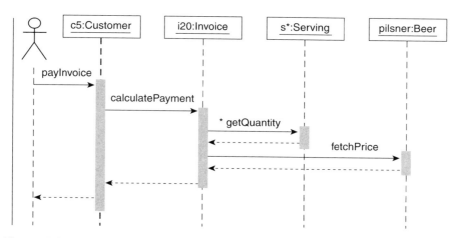

Figure 5-2. **Sequence diagram for the Pay use case.**

Tying It All Together

The remaining dynamic UML view is provided by *sequence diagrams*. Some projects use UML *collaboration diagrams* instead, however, visualizing the same aspects in a class-diagram style layout. Whatever the syntax, we recommend that other stakeholders keep their involvement at a reasonably low level here.[7] With enterprise systems, this is an IT staff exercise; but it results in some questions that call for cooperation with other stakeholders.

In sequence diagrams, we're projecting a "bullet" step from our use-case description on to our class structure and checking how the structure is affected by that particular step of that particular use case. Most people do show the use-case actor as the source triggering the whole sequence here too, in order to increase legibility, as shown in Figure 5-2.[8] Thus, we model *internal interactions* between the cooperating objects.[9] This is crucial because an object

---

[7] On maintenance reasons, we prefer sequence diagrams, even for sketchy, high-level interactions explaining the basics to managers. In addition to those, we recommend collaboration diagrams in user-interface discussions across several use cases, for example, documenting Web-based navigation.

[8] Whether you show the return arrow (the dotted lines between objects) is a matter of style because they can add significant clutter to large diagrams. If you use them at all, we recommend showing the return only if it's conveying some relevant information. For example, "amountDue," whereas a return code that simply means "everything went fine here" can be implied instead, as an "enterprise standard" after each solid arrow. Showing a return that directly affects the course of the sequence is often worthwhile. For example, if a particular return value triggers an "extending" mini-sequence beside the mainstream.

[9] As previously mentioned, objects are dynamic. Sequence diagrams show the dynamic aspect per event, across many objects. Some UML tools are already capable to animate the diagram, thus, making the dynamic aspects more visible.

architecture results in many reusable components (at several levels of granularity – from large/high-level to small – that is, object level) and we need to see how these interact, without having to read program code. With enterprise systems, we simply remember that sequence diagrams provide a view that ties the other views together, thus enabling us to postpone internal interactions in all the other views until now. Otherwise, a split of focus might hit both quality and lead time during use-case and class modeling. Again, projects save effort by keeping the *right issues in the right UML view* (remember keeping the electricity away from the exterior picture of the building).

Strengths

A sequence diagram is easy to understand and to maintain. It specifies how parts of the system cooperate in delivering the functionality stated in a use case. It makes the time dimension visible.

Limitations

A sequence diagram is much easier to draw in a tool than on a whiteboard. As you can guess from its name, it's easiest to maintain if you partition the model into several clear-cut sequences, without "branches" of conditional arrows. Again, a consistent mainstream-before-detail approach saves time here. If you lean toward only one big diagram instead, it tends to grow into a "bush," rather than a sequence, thus becoming difficult to understand and maintain.

Sequence diagrams provide the view *per event and across all objects* involved (objects of several classes), whereas state diagrams *show all events per class*. A simple way of explaining the interrelationship between these two dynamic views is a detailed use-case dialogue-description (bullet list) from a requirement specification of some future animator tool; at the moment, animators have just begun to emerge on the market.[10] Let's call the tool DA-2005 or Double Animator, version 2005. *Double* indicates the tool shall animate – in parallel – the sequence diagram *and* the corresponding state transitions in each corresponding state diagram affected by that particular sequence. So, instead of specifying the tool for only a static, abstract matrix of sequence arrows and state-transition arrows, we specify it to "run" the same matrix logic dynamically and visually, directly in the diagrams.

---

[10] At the moment, Aonix's Object-Animator in Select Enterprise can illustrate dynamically each interaction step between the objects in the sequence diagram (or collaboration diagram). Also, several real-time tools animate state diagrams. With large diagrams and many arrows, this boosts the team's understanding of the dynamic aspects before we move on to implementation. This benefit is similar to one of more advanced process simulators in business process modeling tools.

Use Case: Animate dynamic behavior, stepwise.

> ***Objective/business value:*** ensure understanding and quality of application being developed by animating its proposed behavior, step by step, in both sequence diagrams and state diagrams.

> ***Delivery priority:*** Medium

> ***Steps***

>> **Actor:** Clicks or presses ENTER

>> **System:** Highlights next message arrow in the sequence

>> **A:** Clicks arrowhead of highlighted arrow in the sequence

>> **S:** Displays a small pop-up window on top of arrowhead, showing the *state diagram* of the receiving object's class. Highlights the state-transition arrow corresponding to the message to this object (that is, to the event conveyed by the arrow highlighted in the sequence).

Here, hyperlinks in the "bullets" of use-case descriptions can become the menu. When these kinds of tools are available – we hope in a matter of months, rather than years – the team specifying the system will gain total control of the proposed dynamic behavior and the possibility to "desktop test" it before any program code is written.[11]

Suppose you have a Pay use case, stating the external interactions conveying a card payment into the system for *customer* payment for an *invoice* containing different *servings* of a *liquid*. If these four are affected,[12] the internal interactions look like the sequence diagram in Figure 5-2. An actor triggers the payment sequence (via some user interface[13]), which then asks the

---

[11] The idea of animating dynamic behavior "dynamically" is powerful, natural, and certainly reused. Already in the 1960s, Dutch software-structure pioneer Dijkstra pointed out the limitations of "static" sheets of paper (and lines of code) in describing a process that is dynamic in nature. In the 1980s, one of us took part in a project developing some of the first PC animators for lines of program-code and for diagrams of entity-life structures (so the previous idea of animating several views in parallel is a reused one, too).

[12] In your real-life project, there will be many *more* of them, yet in the same kind of structure. Also, several different objects of the same class might be involved in the same sequence, such as an invoice requesting the serving details from each of its servings (the asterisk-marked arrow in this sequence). During some future discount calculation, this particular invoice might even be asking another, previous invoice, for example, how timely it was paid by this Customer.

[13] This is a card reader in a credit-card terminal or a click button in a Web form. These will be designed in detail later, during user interface design with all the (extra) user interface objects added to the sequence diagram.

THERE'S MORE IN SEQUENCE DIAGRAMS

A complete sequence diagram can show both timing detail and technical detail. For example, messages can be sent directly (synchronously) or posted (asynchronously) without blocking the "sender" by waiting for a direct response. Even some nonfunctional performance requirements might be attached to the arrows and bars of the diagram, such as response time.

As shown with getQuantity in Figure 5–2, an asterisk is used to mark repeated requests.

We can also choose to draw sequence diagrams at several levels of granularity. If, let's say, a CIO asks for a high-level sketch of the basic transaction flow between several subsystems (diagrammed as UML "packages"), then a sequence diagram of packages can help in showing those basics while hiding the detail.

invoice to calculate payment due. Invoice, in turn, retrieves price amount from the particular beer and quantity from each serving (within this particular invoice).

Starting from the mainstream golden case/happy path as usual, the sequence is fairly intuitive as we just read down in the diagram, each arrow mirroring a message, such as a signal, a transaction, a return, and so forth passed between two objects. The vertical lines under the objects are their lifelines. Because time goes from top to bottom in the diagram, each line is as long as the object (shown as its header) is present in the system, that is, from creation to deletion. The thick portion of the lifeline indicates the object is activated (performing an operation or waiting for a return from some other object). The sequence path in the diagram follows the associations, aggregations, and compositions in the class diagram structure.

UML Collaboration Diagrams

Collaboration diagrams tell the same story in a slightly different UML syntax, as shown in Figure 5-3. They make the coupling between objects visible. The class-diagram style of layout is useful in brainstorming with Post-it notes on the whiteboard, whereas sequence diagrams usually win the race in maintenance.

Other UML Diagrams

You might come across some other UML diagrams. These are mainly created by IT staff, so you have only a very general idea of what they're trying to show.

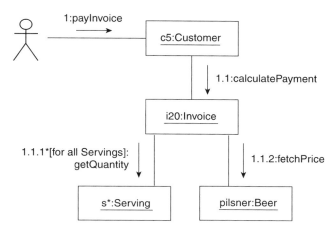

Figure 5-3. **Collaboration diagram for the Pay use case.**

Later, during design and deployment, physical code components can be modeled in UML *component diagrams.*

Where the system-to-be is a mix of both software and hardware, both can be modeled in a UML *deployment diagram* (showing hardware as cubes, with software components on the front of each cube). This is interesting where some specific hardware is an important part of the proposed system, as is often the case in telecom, automatic train control, naval systems, automotive electronics, and so forth. Deployment diagrams were rare for enterprise systems, which exploited common "standard" environments or standardized middleware. But with the explosion of Web-enabled front ends to most enterprise systems, deployment diagrams have become a more frequent technical design document.[14] Generally speaking, adding another couple of diagram types to a project skidding out of control would make it skid *totally* out of control.

Summary

- **State diagrams** model the dynamic aspects *per class,* showing its *life cycle* as *states* and *events* affecting this class. There are two parallel

---

[14] Deployment diagrams can show the location of components on different hardware configurations necessary for Web-based systems. By 2080, Wet-Liquids.com can *show the hardware and software components* together in a deployment diagram, including our Digital *Beverage*-Subscriber Line (D*BSL*) devices (patent applied for).

versions – mainstream and detailed (including less-usual courses of events).

- **Sequence diagrams** model the dynamic aspects *per event* (typically, a use-case step), showing the *interaction* among all the affected objects. These again are at two levels: mainstream and detail (adding "less-usual" courses of events on top of the mainstream, in a manner similar to extend/include between use cases, as discussed in Chapter 3).

- In practice, all dynamic models start from the *mainstream,* that is, the "golden" happy path (which calls for considerable stakeholder involvement), adding less-usual scenarios in the next iteration, which, typically, is an IT-staff exercise.[15]

---

[15] At the moment, standardization work is going on within the Object Management Group, affecting the exact interrelationship of mainstream and detail diagrams. This, in turn, will affect the style of work likely to be practiced here in the future.

Chapter 6

Moving Toward Components

*I**n recent years,** an evolutionary change has occurred in the way modern systems are developed or, perhaps, we should now say "assembled." Instead of building systems from the ground up – designing, construct-ing, and testing every part, thereby incurring time delays and huge costs – modern systems are being assembled from a combination of components to meet the needs of the business. These components or services might have been rented or bought from third-party suppliers, reused from previous sys-tems, or built to provide a special set of services for the solution. The aim is to avoid building most of the solution.

This component-based development strategy can be summed up as *"Reuse before you Buy before you Build."* It's the new approach to meet the needs of tomorrow. Interestingly, the UML, as well as 99 percent of this book, works fine with any of these alternatives, including a combination of alternatives. This chapter explains the background of many seemingly odd questions raised by IT people, which might seem to be too early in the pro-ject. As we show, components can early on play a key role in the bid/pro-posal stage of a project.

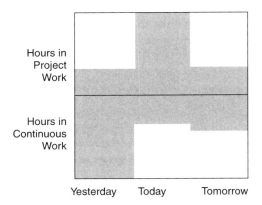

Figure 6-1. **Yesterday – today – tomorrow effort matrix.**

Yesterday's development approach was for large amounts of time and effort spent in developing *basic* parts of the system architecture,[1] for example, visual controls, communications interfacing, and so forth with a smaller amount of time and effort spent in project-related activities, that is, delivering solutions, as shown in Figure 6-1. Today's development approach reuses many components that were once built and maintained by your IT organization and the effort has moved to working mainly on projects to deliver solutions. But little cross-project or cross-product sharing of components occurs. Too often, every project is an "island." And, still, despite their best intentions, it takes too long for software developers to build the systems. They can't write code any faster with the present set of concepts and resources, and they've reached the limits of many development tools.

Tomorrow's development approach[2] – and today's forerunners' approach – using components reduces our project workload because most of the work is component-related, cross-project/cross-product activities. We try to develop components *once* to a high quality, thus minimizing the effort of writing the same functionality many times for future solutions. This, then, meets our need to improve productivity – otherwise, the lost earnings through late delivery of products dramatically affect the bottom line of all organizations.

One way to consider the differences between the approaches is with the analogy of restaurants and cafeterias.

---

[1] One of the authors remembers having to write drum storage access software before he could use a new computer. This was in the early 1970s. The other one of us remembers writing many parts of an online transaction monitor before he could make the system receive data from end –users, which occurred in the late 1970s.

[2] The idea of "yesterday vs. today" is a reused component. It originates from Objectory (Lars Wiktorin, currently at IT-Plan). We added the vision of a configure-and-deploy "tomorrow" to it.

In a restaurant, diners choose from a menu prepared by expert chefs. This menu reflects their requirements: what is in season, which combinations are popular, what can be offered in different ways to reduce waste, and so forth. Diners can only choose from these set combinations; things not on the menu are unavailable. This is a form of *supply-side control,* similar to the old style of software development where the IT department controlled all activities.

In contrast, the cafeteria (or the smorgasbord) offers a selection of foods prepared by experts that are laid out and replenished regularly. Diners now choose any combination to suit their own requirements, that is, they create their own meals. They might need expert help, say, in carving some of the ingredients but, if competent, they can undertake the task themselves. This is *demand-side control,* which reflects the new style of development found in most knowledge industries.

Not everyone likes to eat in a cafeteria, however, as the choice might still be limited and the offerings of poor quality. Whereas, when ordering through a waiter, special instructions can be given to the cooks, and then sometimes fulfilled on delivery or sometimes misunderstood and not fulfilled. Cafeterias require an attentive customer and a joint effort in configuring the meal.

The same is true for component reuse. Attentive management and attentive stakeholders are needed to ensure that components don't become stale and that a best-match configuration is selected. Of course, the smorgasbord is an excellent principle of quickly meeting heterogeneous requirements of customers from a variety of niches (allergy, special diet, vegetarian, children, curious tourist, and so forth). Many e-enterprises call this principle "Configure and Buy."[3] Having the right components ready upfront enables them to do in minutes what used to take weeks or months with traditional restaurant approaches.

This is only the beginning of the story, however. In the knowledge industry, change is added on top of all this. On top of *differences* among customers/stakeholders already in the *first version,* the requirements are frequently *changed* as the "meal" is being configured and consumed. Again, meeting variance over time is more straightforward and cost-effective with configurable components. Configured systems tend to keep a rather constant reconfiguration cost, whereas maintenance costs of proprietary solutions tend to accelerate in an uncontrollable manner after a few upgraded versions. This is a major point, which is quite different from many other sectors of industry: whereas adding a fifth engine to a Jumbo jet is considered a non-option, software functionality is frequently (sometimes also fundamentally) altered and *upgraded after delivery* and regular use. In our opinion, this point was paid too little attention during the pre-UML era.

---

[3] Witness the recent explosion of interest in Web services.

WHAT IS A COMPONENT?

Several competing definitions exist for a component, but they share common characteristics. Such characteristics include components as units of runable, deployable software that offer services (high-level "operations") via interfaces, using standard fittings
(a standard communications technology), and are assembled with other components
to realize a business solution.

Several UML diagrams deal with components. The most general construct is a UML
package, shown in Figure B6-1. Packages can be used for several purposes. Often,
packages are used for grouping low-level constructs into high-level components.* The
most common relationship between packages is a dependency (see the dotted arrow
in Figure B6-1). The most commonly used stereotype of this dependency is «communicate», that is, requests sent to the other components to obtain help from them in
completing the tasks of the component sending the request.**

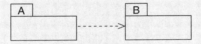

***Figure B6-1.* UML packages (components).**

---

* Packages can even be nested – in packages on the next "level," and next, up to subsystems or systems. As you can guess from the name, *package* is primarily a packaging technique in design, rather
than an analysis tool. As mentioned in Chapter 4, the path of reasoning in analysis is middle-out
rather than top-down.

** Other stereotypes of dependencies can be more "technical," for example, compilation dependen-
cies when the computer requires all the interdependent components as input at the same time, i.e.,
"all of it or none of it" (for compiling or linkage). In "design to configure," we can also choose to diagram inclusion/exclusion dependencies between components on various levels. Later on, these can
become rules to be applied automatically by a configurator package while "assembling" our system.

Thus, having the right components ready makes both version 1 projects
and upgrade projects lean, as shown in Figure 6-1.

Components Communicate with Everyone

From the requirement specification point of view, components offer a more
powerful and predefined *way of communication.* Instead of the drawn-out
process of specifying each and every detail of the requirements we can just
identify a known component or specify the services that we want. In many
sectors of industry, this has resulted in an improved efficiency within the
sales process of the forerunners of component-based product architectures.
Thus, the component approach itself is a key strategy in extending your
market share by covering more segments and niches. This important mecha-

nism deserves more attention on the component agenda – which in high-tech enterprises generally tends to focus on product and production.

The communicative power of a component is similar to a technical term in natural language: if a financial analyst mentions something like "a black Monday scenario" to a colleague, they probably save pages of detailed text because the scenario has previously been analyzed, described, and labeled. So, if you talk about the Accounts Department (as a high-level software component in, say, a Web shop), you can easily mention the services you expect for your solution, for example, take a credit-card payment, check the "hot list" for defrauders, and alert when accounts are overdue.

Where solutions are *assembled* from bought-in parts (and where they are wholly *constructed* from the ground up by the development teams), the specification work and business analysis don't simply walk away. It's critical for the stakeholders to specify the (business) services required in the new solution and to discuss the resulting component models to ensure these services will be delivered.

Specifying Components for Wet-Liquids.com

If we return to our 2080 example for Wet-Liquids.com, we can identify a number of components that represent the obvious business elements: sales department, product, distribution, Accounts Department, and customer. These components are at a "near-top" level.[4] Large component libraries, such as IBM's SanFrancisco (SF), are typically at *several levels of granularity*. Both in SF and in OMG's view of components, our "product" and "customer" (see Figure 6-2) are standard examples of so-called *business objects*. They're far above the technical level, but still frequent in most kinds of systems.

Distribution (in Figure 6-2) is an example of SF's top level, originally called *application frameworks* or SanFrancisco Towers, that is, "Lego-brick towers," assembled of business objects (other examples at this level are financials, HRM, or manufacturing). Figure 6-2 shows these components, as well as another one added within the Accounts Department to deal with the online credit-card banking service. This is an example of wrapping components up in other components (or *nesting*). The dotted line shows the dependencies between the components,[5] that is, sales needs to know about all the other components, but all the other components don't need to know about

---

[4] Some other people might choose to make each activity of a process a component (to increase configurability), which isn't at "top," yet is at quite a high level.

[5] These dependencies are of the «communicate» stereotype, to be exact: technically, the sales-department component will be sending requests to the other components whenever necessary.

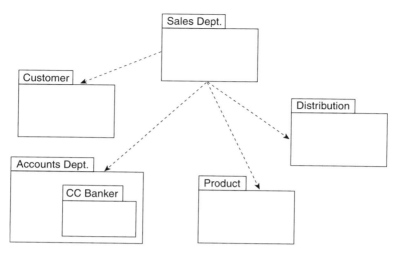

Figure 6-2. **Example components for Wet-Liquids.com.**

each other. If we reconfigure the system to run some new process in addition to the current order process, then we probably just add some more dependencies here.

Once these components are identified, we now outline the *responsibilities* allocated to each one:

- **Sales Department:** responsible for processing each customer's drink request (listing products, validating choices, submitting orders to distribution), managing customer subscriptions, and issuing sales orders.

- **Customer:** responsible for recording personal and subscription details, knowing their own account balance and payment status, and holding a history of sales.

- **Product:** responsible for knowing details of the product including restrictions (for example, age/alcohol), providing pricing and discounts, recording stock levels, and monitoring the shelf-life status.

- **Distribution:** responsible for managing the product inventory and distribution channels *[sic]*, accepting new products from suppliers, dispensing the product to customers, and reporting the status of the distribution channels.

- **Accounts Department:** responsible for issuing customer statements, collecting payments, updating customer payment records, and reporting defaulters.

- **CC Banker:** responsible for validating credit cards and charging payments to customer credit-card accounts; an online authorization service.

These are high-level components. Some of them can be bought as components, some can be rented as Web services, some can be bought as parts of a package, some can be reused from previous projects, and some can be developed now.

From this "Lego kit," we can, in principle, configure a process chain, for example, the order cycle. Now, suppose we have a merger a few years later, resulting in a new marketing policy. Because of this, before adding a customer address to the mailing list of the sales department component, the current credit rating of the customer must be checked automatically to invest Wet-Liquids.com's sales efforts in customers with proper liquid assets. The dependency between the sales department and accounts is already in place. We simply adjust our sequence diagram (activating the credit-rating check in the Accounts Department component) and reconfigure the system. The credit-rating checker component can be nested within the Accounts Department from the beginning or easily purchased otherwise, for example, from Dun & Bradstreet or from a component broker.

In fact, this modest change can evolve into a rather extreme example of *Reuse before Buy before Build*. The traditional build and deploy approach ("supply-side" control) could easily spend weeks specifying and designing this upgrade. A new proprietary rating component could take years to develop and another year to fine-tune, especially with business-to-business customers. If you're serious about making computers interpret and analyze complex financial information (producing credible, realistic credit ratings), you need a lot[6] of financial data, smart information-mining tools, a couple of sophisticated knowledge bases, a panel of credit-rating experts to keep the knowledge current, plus a skilled team of IT people. In our humble opinion, reusing a component of proven quality developed by someone else is more realistic.

Impact of the Component-Based Approach

"Reuse before you Buy before you Build" means components might already exist as part of existing solutions and can be reused in the planned system.

---

[6] Although the results, i.e., the ratings per company, might fit on a CD-ROM or three, the raw material necessary for producing them can be hundreds of gigabytes of financial databases.

Purchase Focus	OTS-Package	Components and Services	Tools and Services
Specification Effort	Critical	Critical	Critical
Design Effort	Low Intensity	Medium Intensity	High Intensity

Figure 6-3. **Different aspects on the scale between buying and building solutions.**

Or, it can be bought to fit your requirements, configured, if necessary. Building them is the last resort if no components are available that fit the solution. Figure 6-3 shows we can have a scale between the buying and building, which shows the different nature of the development processes; whichever is used, *specification* is still critical on all of them.

Buying Components
Buying components is attractive to most organizations, but both advantages and disadvantages exist with bought components. The advantages include:

- Cost savings, especially for maintenance because this is transferred to the component supplier.

- Engineered to meet the requirements of the reuser.

- Earlier payback because only the cost of the components is to be recovered. This usually makes projects leaner and (therefore) their start procedure is much shorter.

- Manpower savings because they can be deployed onto other projects.

- Greater range of capabilities, for example, new service offerings, such as our previous credit-rating example.

- Technology leverage giving the capability to enter new domains, for example, mobile 3G/GPRS interfacing.

- Reliability – provided previous use on other projects.

- Documentation[7] that encourages reuse. You know up front what you're going to get.

But difficulties exist with bought components:

- Little use in the application for (reusing) the components; for example, they might offer great screen controls that you don't need.

---
[7] You would expect or demand such documentation to be in the UML format!

- Delays might occur in the procurement of the component. It's the supplier's schedule, not yours. *Control lies with the supplier* and not with your organization. If the supplier drops the component, problems in upgrades and maintenance must be dealt with by your own staff.

- In-house expertise is needed to reuse the components.

- In-house improvements might also be required, giving a potential maintenance hazard.

- New role of *component buyer* feels inconvenient both to the traditional buyer – skilled in buying coffee, furniture, and pencils – and to the software-people – skilled in developing components, rather than in buying them.

When to Buy or Build
In deciding when to buy or build, the focus needs to be on the benefits to the user of the component.

- What is it worth (value) to the user?

- Is the user willing to pay to have the best version of this component or to have one that's minimally sufficient?

- What is the impact if the component is *not* provided?

- How big, stable, service-minded, and reliable is the component vendor?

As a general example, let's take the colored housing for the rear light on a car. This is obviously needed, so we can't drop the requirement, but does it need to be the best available? The car buyer wouldn't be willing to pay a premium for a rear light, so the choice is for one that's minimally sufficient. Car designers then look at the available housings and design the vehicle's rear end accordingly. If the case was for a new high-performance fuel-cell engine for which the car buyer was willing to pay a premium, then the car design would be driven by both the engine and the engine space.

Reusing Components

When considering reuse, it's necessary to be aware of the differences among pluggable, customizable, and configurable components.

Pluggable components support the "black-box" concept: you know what the component does, but not how it does it. The component has hard edges specified as well-defined software interfaces. It can be likened to Lego bricks for children. Each brick has a well-defined interface or connecting part that will fit any other brick with the same style of connection. Lego firmly deemphasizes *how* to do things in favor of *what* to do. Lego bricks are very easy to use, but very hard to design and build[8] to ensure they fit together well. Users of components (and Lego bricks) expect a useful set of artifacts to undertake some task and look to the expert component maker to provide this useful set. For this expert, the components must be designed and constructed to meet both the requirements of their reusers and to an extremely high quality. Lego connections (fittings) show clearly why *interfaces* are key in modern software architectures.[9]

Customizable components are the form of adaptive reuse, that is, what to do and how to do it. The components have soft edges and soft contents, which allows the reusers to adjust the components to fit their exact requirements. Such components are easier to design and construct because they only need to provide a generic set of features and let the reusers modify accordingly. Such components, however, are difficult and expensive to maintain because any updates must be examined for the impact on the customized component and any new works retested. This can occur any number of times throughout the lifespan of a system, making a continual coordination of system versions and component versions necessary.

Configurable components are pluggable components that can have their behavior or data changed through well-defined mechanisms. These still remain a "black box" because the configurator doesn't know how the internals of the component have been changed.

The "boundary" between component-based development and "packages" has been growing quite fuzzy recently – a trend of which IBS is an example. As former packages evolve into "UML-packages" of configurable components, the enterprise buying the package can either use it right away as a large, single, off-the-shelf package (just as before) or intermix components from several sources, including its own legacy components. Again, wherever we are on this new scale between "buy" and "build" (Figure 6-3), the specification work and business analysis doesn't simply disappear. Even in the tra-

---

[8] In fact, the molds for the bricks are cut on expensive machines that are accurate to a micron by using spark-erosion technology.

[9] Consequently, in addition to UML, which is a "specification and design-time" standard, most OMG "deployment-time" standards for multiplatform systems are published in terms of standard interface definitions. These tell the software industry which services shall be provided to other systems (or other components) through each interface – without the detail of implementing those services behind that interface. This focus on interfaces makes the system architecture reconfigurable and resilient to change, by "insulating" most changes *inside* each component from the rest.

ditional off-the-shelf case, despite all the design outside the buyer's enterprise shrinking the whole project, we still need a requirement specification and we still need to understand the essence of all those UML diagrams.

Building a Component Library

Considering every component that exists for reuse is neither possible nor practical. The first step is a decision on which reusable components you want to manage as reusable assets. This means considering the structure of the business, the needs of the existing or planned projects, your computer architecture, and the opinions of potential reusers.

Components that support the business are the most useful. These can be found in the structure of your business. Organizational boundaries show independent business units that have responsibility for creating, delivering, and supporting its own products. While each unit will have its own requirements, these can be met by local reusable components or supplied from components that are organization-wide – that is, sharable across many units. Another approach is to look for different levels of generality. There will be components of interest to any business, those of interest to any company within the industry, and, finally, those specific to a company. For example, screen widgets are useful to all businesses, tax rules are useful to many companies, and a polymer paint-mixing recipe is useful to a specific company.

When considering the need of existing or planned projects a number of strategies can be used. One strategy, called *domain analysis,* attempts to understand the fundamental abstractions in a given area, whether business- or technology-related. If a general domain model can be produced, then this will be useful to multiple projects. The outcome of a domain analysis is the identification of reuse opportunities across applications in a domain, for example, personnel, inventory, accounts receivable, and so forth. Another approach is *on-the-fly identification.* Faced with short-term deadlines and an aggressive attitude to exploit new technology, a number of projects are started simultaneously, hampering any attempts at domain analysis. In this environment, reuse is handled with a just-in-time attitude, projects helping each other through assigning team members to cross-project teams.

Can I Trust This Component?

If you're going to rely on this component in your new system, you'll want some guarantee from the supplier. Certification ensures that the reusable components meet some level of quality. This engenders trust in the component when you can be confident that an independent evaluation of the component has been done. But what happens if that process is slow or components are needed promptly? Most successful certification schemes issue *levels of certification* with the reusable component, ranging from 0: just arrived, so use with care, to 5: used successfully in at least four other systems.

Sharing Components in Your Organization

Components do *not* come out of thin air. As in many other industries, the following scale (in addition to Figure 6-2) illustrates clearly how top management becomes increasingly involved in the adoption process of software components and standards. Middle-sized software houses became the forerunners, mainly because of the sustained attention paid to components by their top management. Reusability starts from object technology and the UML, whereas reuse in real life, that is, component sharing, starts from well-informed, dedicated, and pushy top management.

Our rather informal scale of component-sharing maturity provides a hint on the state of affairs in practice within our project and our enterprise:

0. **Sharing *within* a team:** a dedicated person or three with hazy roles and management.

1. **Sharing *within* a family** of products or projects.

2. **Sharing *across* families** of products or projects, of components developed within the firm. Staying profitable for almost seven decades in a tough market, truck maker Scania is a forerunner of this level of sharing. For example, some 80 percent of a bus platform's components are reused truck designs.

3. **Sharing *across* a group** of companies. On several continents, carmakers within the VW Group are among the forerunners having used a common component management system for many years.

4. **Sharing *with* a competitor.** Some firms seem to succeed here; others try the next stage. For example, several car makers have achieved this higher level of sharing and seem happy with that. On the other hand, although collaborating for several years, ERP and CRM-vendors IBS and Mapics proceeded to the next stage anyway.

5. **Sharing *within* a sector of industry.** The twenty-first century "top performance": enterprises sharing standard components with all firms interested. Typically, as the component activity grows, it becomes a business and profit stream in its own right. In software, there are component libraries and frameworks, complete object versions of ERPs,

open-source software, and so forth. In the mid nineties, Swedish ERP-vendor IBS provided some key ideas and experts to IBM, triggering a large-scale Shared Framework project (SF, SanFrancisco). Later, having provided several thousands of components at several levels of granularity, SF spun off into an IBM company on its own with 500+ customers using the framework on a royalty basis. Currently, SF is the Business Components[10] part of IBM's Websphere® product suite.

Thus, even when developing one-of-a-kind systems, a one-of-a-kind cost level isn't necessary.[11] The ROI of component sharing is good, to say the least,[12] but a threshold exists because of the investment and the focus necessary on entry. Firms relying on a few technical enthusiasts are stuck at level 0, R&D managers cope at levels 1, 2, and 3, whereas levels 4 and 5 imply CEO commitment.[13]

Avoiding the Traps

Again, there are some common pitfalls here and, again, staying away from them seems much cheaper. This time, the list of traps is rather generic.

Just-a-New-Diagram

The UML provides several semi-technical diagrams. Package diagrams, component diagrams, and deployment diagrams mirror what we need to know at a technical/architectural level. These also prevent people from force-fitting high-level components (such as searchers, reporters, and so forth) somewhere else, typically into use cases (as mentioned earlier, a use case usually spans across *several* components, so use cases aren't the right place). They also enable us to show an overall system structure quickly, including some technical components at a high, zoomed-out level.

However, the UML techniques alone aren't enough to take us to the top of the previous scale.

---

[10] The new WebSphere® Business Components version of SF conforms to a software component standard (Enterprise Java Beans™) coordinated by Sun. See *http://java.sun.com/products/ejb/training.html*.

[11] Similar sharing initiatives seem to be under way elsewhere. The trick here is simply to avoid writing/making the program code, by reusing shared components instead, industry-wide and world-wide.

[12] WebSphere Business Components cut development time by more than half.

[13] The comparison of generalist and specialist methodologies in the introduction provides only a hint on a method's overall ambition regarding high-level components. This scale, on the other hand, is much more focused on the current state of an enterprise.

Brainware Is a Beautiful Trap

At the moment, among the "would-be-nice-ifs" of software tools the fundamental missing feature is *intelligent configurators*. Whereas Scania's truck-
order process has been supported by smart sales configurators for several
decades, the software industry itself is still mostly low-tech on this point.
That's not logical because configurators are the harvesting machinery, in a
sense, for all the benefits of object technology and of any component-based
architecture.

However, now that the OMG has a format standard for UML-model interchange across tools,[14] even configurator vendors can join the UML race.[15]

Configurators will also make it much easier to reconfigure an enterprise
system immediately after a major business change, so such tools certainly
deserve to be closely watched and thoroughly tested during the next few
years. With other configurable products in, for example, complex manufacturing, there has been quite a long takeoff run. Configurators didn't pay off
until a culture of "design to configure" became rooted in the R&D department and spread throughout the enterprise. Unsurprisingly, previous product architectures, not designed to be configured by computer programs,
turned out to be hardly configurable at all. This stepwise start procedure
indicates it's high time for the software industry to enter, starting the first
iteration right away.

Remember, *configuration management* tools are *not* sales configurators.
These tools basically keep track of existing configurations, most often
already made by people "by hand."

Beware of Lawyers!

A major trap is the protection of your legal interests when you buy and sell
reusable components. Software legislation doesn't consist of a unique set of
dedicated laws, but is an adaptation from different, old, well-established
fields of law, for example, copyright law. One of the major complexities
when considering the legal aspects is the source of the various components
that make up a system. Components might have been bought from third

---

[14] The XML Metadata Interchange (XMI) is a standard that makes it possible for teams
using different UML tools with different internal data formats to cooperate and exchange
their UML diagrams.

[15] As in other knowledge industries, a quick-'n-dirty configurator prototype is a non-option
in the long run. Rather than simple things in Visual Basic, we need *smart* software tools to
process component lists of potentially thousands of components at several levels of granularity viable in millions of possible combinations – yet capturing and correctly interpreting
all their interdependencies, constraints, inclusion/exclusion rules, and so forth. When these
tools are finally connected to the Web (or otherwise customer-enabled), they become
extremely interesting to the sales manager.

parties, extended to increase the functionality, and then further extended and paid for as part of a client contract. Three levels of component are here: bought with licensed use, developed to include trade secret, and passed by copyright to a client.

When approaching components for protection, three legal categories can be identified.

- strategic knowledge confined to organization

- non-strategic knowledge with commercial value

- non-strategic knowledge of little value

This gives a clue to what level of protection you might seek. Care is also needed if your organization delivers reusable components. Binary code and user documentation would require a different level of protection than when the component comprised the specification, source code, and so forth. At the same time, your organization also has to take competitors into account in some niches, including components like freeware, shareware, and open source software.

Automating the Bid Process

CIOs (and sales managers of software firms) need to be rather open-minded on configurators and component-based architectures. In the knowledge industry, hitting dates in tenders and contests is essential. Surprisingly, considering the levels of automation in today's production and the short supply of skilled sales engineers, it's amazing how *rarely* automated the early steps of the high-tech order cycle are.

As mentioned in this book's introduction, workflow-oriented, standard BPR cases typically provide a perfect solution to the wrong problem. Rather, by using knowledge as supplied in design-to-configure components and with intelligent software tools, long-term efficiency can be attained.

A few years ago, British (Benchmark UK) and American (Gartner US) industry surveys presented – fairly similar – interesting findings on the bidding process. In complex software and telecom, a UK industry average was 1,000+ working hours per bid. With a hit rate slightly above 35 percent, this meant some 3,000 hours per real order.[16]

Thus, from the various points of view of development, production, deployment, and sales, in particular, all the effort put into components and

---

[16] When these figures are shown to representatives from large European defense and electronics industries, they report that the figures might even be an underestimate.

configurability is definitely worthwhile. This effort pays off in both foreseen and unforeseen ways. During times when a shortage exists of skilled personnel, successful bids can still be created using the captured knowledge in the components. And, in times of cost-consciousness and severe price competition, improvements in development productivity and exploitation of existing proven components ensures your bids meet these constraints, and the cost estimates underlying the bid are realistic.

Consequently, any enterprise strategy (and practice) must cover component issues, including software components. In a knowledge industry, our enterprise might build its entire business idea on components, growing into a component vendor, a component buyer/assembler (that is, component-based package vendor), a tool vendor, an adviser, a component broker, and so on. Most often, components are key to any knowledge-intensive business idea.

Summary

Components, component-based development methods, and techniques is the way forward for the future. Software development is essentially a knowledge industry and not a craft industry. Software development has to think in terms of the successes of using and *reusing* components in an enterprise. With system development departments in several countries, you can have a "cooperative race" in component sharing similar to the one among the car makers within the VW group, where a car design employing, say, 60 percent of shared components can be regarded as a "winner."[17]

The point is, unsurprisingly, to design and build each component only *once*, making it really *good* instead.

---

[17] Although there's not extremely tough competition among the brands of the whole VW group in the marketplace. In a sense, this is a race *within* the same team (and a profitable race, for all parties).

Chapter 7

Mapping from Classes to Data Models

*D*ata modeling has been covered thoroughly for decades. Like class diagrams, it provides a structural view. Unlike class diagrams, data modeling omits business-level operations that the proposed system will perform. Most often, it also omits some key relationships, such as generalization, despite the fact that various data-model notations for generalization have been around for almost two decades. Because most data models are on a design level, they already take into account some restrictions posed by the underlying implementation technology (data tables).

Strengths
Data models cope well with the data to be stored in the bottom layer of a system. Therefore, data modeling is a technique suitable later on, during design. The mapping to data models enables modern object-oriented systems to use ordinary relational database engines, which are standard in enterprise systems. In practice, brief previews with Database Administrators are a good idea to coordinate legacy and other systems with our models to come. By the time data modeling becomes really interesting in our project, we already have a more technical focus.

Limitations
Data models omit most of the behavior and business logic. Also, what data modelers call *constraints* or *rules* typically turns out to mean special data-related ones (such as rules of referential integrity across data tables), whereas UML includes a more versatile and powerful standard for declaring complex business logic, the UML Object Constraint Language (OCL). At the specification stage, a data focus is likely to trigger a rush into design solutions, resulting in the full-plate syndrome – in other words, overloading everyone with decisions on the technical detail of the system.

Use Appropriate Diagrams and Standards

We strongly recommend a layered system architecture or at least a layered way of thinking here. This makes understanding where UML fits in (the business logic layer) and where data models fit in (the bottom layer) much easier. Data models in the form of entity relationship (ER) diagrams have frequently been used *instead of* UML class diagrams, rather than as a *complementary view:* the data-centric view. Such approaches are likely to result in a system much less resilient to change and in databases too specific to a single system because of a hazy (or nonexistent) business-logic tier, making the database contain some of that logic instead. Unsurprisingly, data models will do *on data,* but not on the rest: the system behavior, the business logic, the program logic, and so forth.

The OMG has recently adopted a vendor-independent standard for data modeling and database creation[1] to make life easier for an enterprise with several database platforms.

People are also using variants of the UML class icon, "stereotyped" for data modeling as «Table» or «T». Among the abundance of notations and techniques here, however, Erwin®[2] tools for ER models have been near de facto standard, so many UML tools offer an Erwin bridge for ER-diagram generation from UML class diagrams.[3] This facility greatly simplifies design, implementation, and upgrade by an automatic linkage to data. Taking advantage of this facility, however, takes a good knowledge of both UML and data models, as well as of the mapping techniques between object and

---

[1] The Common Warehouse Metamodel (CWM) *(www.omg.org/technology/cwm/index.htm).*

[2] By Computer Associates, *www.cai.com.*

[3] Modern UML tools provide an automated mapping from the business logic layer to the data layer by *generating* the data model in, for instance, Erwin, as well as by generating the database schema in SQL's Data Definition Language from standard UML class diagrams. The bulk of the work is done by the tool. The modelers make only the high-level decisions on the structure of the data model.

relational technology.[4] The three following alternatives show the main options we have at the conceptual level. The issue of database mapping is wider and deeper than outlined here, though, especially as we move on into design of tables and keys.

Mapping Relationships

Whereas computer program structures are generated from UML in a straight-forward manner, data models and database schemas require several decisions to be made up front. The easier part is mapping the attributes from classes on to columns of tables, although some complex attributes, such as a world map or a video shot to be used on the Web, usually also require further decomposition or additional work. The trickier part is the structure of the model because a necessary conceptual transform takes place from UML class diagrams to data models whose structures also match the low end: table lines and references between table lines (to be stored as so-called foreign keys). Generalization relationships (see Chapter 4) deserve special attention during the transform. Conceptually, we choose from three alternatives when mapping UML generalizations to a data model (some UML-mapping tools[5] ask us to select one alternative up-front):

1. *Make one to one.* Generate one data-model entity or one database table, per UML class. Each UML generalization becomes a one-to-one association between tables, connecting each table line to its corresponding line in the table of its superclass. This alternative is quite straightforward and resilient to upgrades of the class diagram.[6]

2. *Roll down.* In principle, generate one bigger entity, or one table, per "leaf " at the bottom level of the UML tree (the class hierarchy)[7] and include even the data from all superclasses of that leaf into the same table. This makes one table of each *UML-generalization path,* including

---

[4] The technical knowledge necessary to make the right decisions here includes bidirectional association, many-to-many associations, referential integrity (with one to one, one to many, and aggregation), design of primary keys and foreign keys (especially with UML-class generalization relationships), logical access facilities provided by the database engine, such as indices (especially for many-to-many and bidirectional one-to-many associations).

[5] This is likely to be simplified in the near future when SQL 3 becomes an ANSI standard for databases.

[6] With some database engines, however, this complicates the update of data in an individual object stored as lines in several tables. This is because, at the moment, many database engines can't update several tables automatically from temporary data (i.e., from a view or from a cursor).

[7] To be more exact, for each class having real objects, i.e., isn't *abstract.*

data from each class level on that path. Each individual object corresponds to exactly one row in exactly one table. This alternative might be fine as long as searches rarely regard a superclass, while answering requests, such as "count all liquids," becomes much more technically complicated. This alternative also generates redundant, repeated, superfluous, more-of-the-same, column definitions in the table headers. For example, in Figure 7-1 the definitions of "price" and all future attributes of the UML class called Liquid (the "root" level of the UML tree) must now be defined and maintained in all *five* tables of its leaf subclasses (Detergents, Beers, Juices, Colas, Pepsis). This is at the definition level *only* (or the "table header level," the schema), however. No redundancy occurs in the rows of data being actually stored in those tables because each individual object is of exactly one UML subclass (or leaf), thus belonging to exactly one table. For example, we don't store *price values* of various beer-objects in various tables – we simply store all those in rows of the Beers table (and nowhere else).

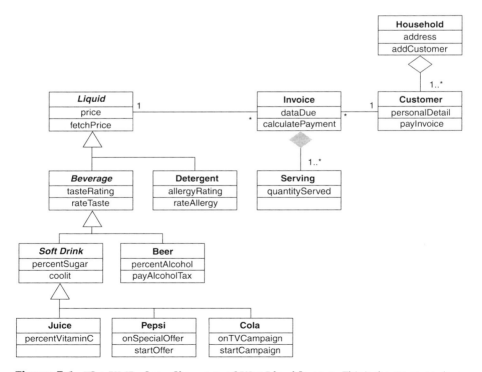

Figure 7-1. **The UML class diagram of Wet-Liquids.com.** This is the structure view.

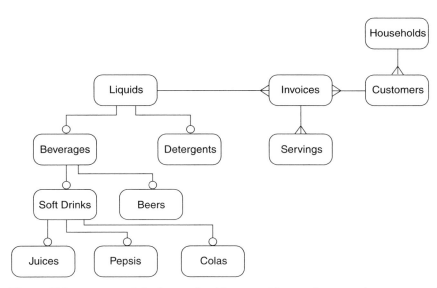

Figure 7-2. **Data model of Wet-Liquids.com. Alternative 1:** *Make one to one,* which means one data-model entity, or table, per UML class. Straightforward from most points of view, except data updates from complete objects (implying data from several tables at a time).

3. *Roll up.* In principle, generate one big pseudo-entity, or one table, per UML class tree and include data from all classes in that tree. This alternative might be fine, as long as searches rarely regard a subclass (requests like "count colas" take long searches in an extremely large table). In addition, advanced UML structures combining all three kinds of UML relationships will look like relationships within the same data table, although they span several UML classes. In each row – depending on the class of the particular object whose data are stored in the row – null values will be in the columns that aren't applicable to that class. So, here, unlike in the previous alternative two, we'll be facing redundant null values[8] in *each* of the stored rows of this long table, resulting in some waste of storage. This alternative is technically possible, therefore, but hardly comprehensible, especially in upgrade time. Database administrators generally agree this alternative is the "last resort," and rather questionable both in the object community and in the data-modeling community.

---

[8] On practical reasons, there will also be an extra column containing a "type flag" or "class flag," telling the class of the object stored in a particular row.

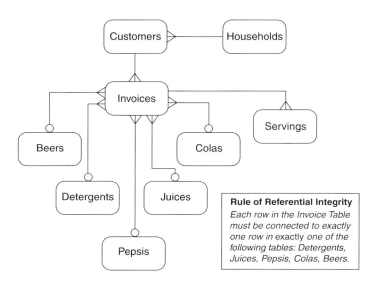

Rule of Referential Integrity
*Each row in the Invoice Table
must be connected to exactly
one row in* exactly *one of the
following tables: Detergents,
Juices, Pepsis, Colas, Beers.*

***Figure 7-3.* Data model of Wet-Liquids.com. Alternative 2: Roll down,** which
means one bigger entity, or table, per "leaf " in the UML class tree, including the data from
its superclasses into the same table. This might be fine as long as searches rarely regard a
superclass. As we can see here, for example, no such table as Liquids exists, so a query
regarding Liquids triggers searches in five tables (Detergents, Juices, Pepsis, Colas, and
Beers).

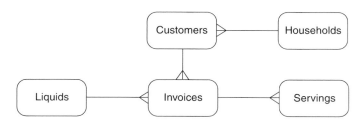

***Figure 7-4.* Data model of Wet-Liquids.com. Alternative 3: Roll up,** which
means one huge table per UML class tree, including the data from all its classes into the
same table – thus, Liquids contains attributes from the UML class Liquid, plus from its subclasses (Detergent, Beverage, Beer, Soft drink, Juice, Pepsi, and Cola) – altogether, data from
eight classes in one table. Use very sparingly. This is impractical in requests regarding any
class except Liquid and quite hopeless in maintenance.

In Figures 7-2 through 7-4, we mapped our class diagram (Figure 7-1) of Wet-Liquids.com on a data model. The ER notation here is slightly different from UML:

- UML 0..1 corresponds to a ring symbol.

- UML * corresponds to a fork symbol.

- UML 1 corresponds to a straight line.

The path of reasoning here is also different. Also, remember we're modeling only the data and not the behavior.

Summary

- *Data models* provide the data view at the bottom tier of a layered-system architecture, in a slightly different notation.

- The *mapping* from UML to data models requires several decisions to be made up front. A conceptual transform occurs from UML class diagrams to a semi-technical view, which is closer to the underlying storage.

- Among all the architectural and technical *decisions* to be made here, the major one is the choice among Make one to one, Roll down, and Roll up.

Chapter 8
Concluding Remarks

Think Big, Start Small, and Sustain the Effort

Most people agree that analysis occurs only when the domain expert is in the room.[1] In our experience, in addition to being present, experts are also supposed to understand the language "spoken" in the room. The language problem has often turned out to be even bigger than that of business-travel logistics. The UML, however, provides many powerful tools to make yourself understood in the room, which come in handy for the frequent visitor. By writing this book, we simply seized the opportunity and packaged much of the substance in a lightweight manner for this purpose.

Implementing UML models (and tools) to specify requirements doesn't take much time. Employing them in a practical approach preshrunk to fit your type of systems takes more training days and practical experience. Finally, adopting a component approach throughout the enterprise can take years of sustained effort, but it's definitely worthwhile.[2]

---

[1] This concise wording originates from Brad Kain.

[2] Scania has fine-tuned its modular truck architecture for 50 years. Industry leaders simply don't emerge overnight.

UML Under Time Constraints

We believe the lightweight style of this book makes it possible for experts from many other areas to approach practical, basic UML. A frequent guest to the landscape of software can view this as a *phrase book* for the journey, keeping grammar detail at a minimum because many good grammar books already exist for this modeling language.

At the same time, we've provided some hints on cooperation with the hosts and on what parts of the language a guest typically becomes involved with in practice. The basic guideline is this: *focus on your part of the job*. Provide clear input and answers to others' questions, so they can focus on their jobs.

Good *communication in a common language based on a world standard* saves time, avoids misunderstanding, and reduces effort. As the boundaries of systems and components are made visible, the same thing happens to boundaries between roles in a project. Intercommunication becomes more standardized and targeted, both in the project and in the product. The viewpoint throughout this book is more one of *every day* modeling work than one of planning or managing a development project, which is yet another area that's well covered by other books.

Figure 8-1 shows the degree of involvement of nonprogrammers who specify the system and the programmers who develop the system. Over the past decade, the boundary line in the figure has been *moving* slowly from left to right. Business experts are becoming more involved in the modeling stages. Standardization, in general, and UML, in particular, facilitate this trend.

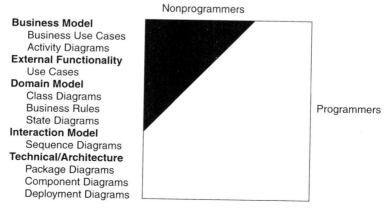

Figure 8-1 **Degree of involvement.**

- **Business model:** business use cases, activity diagrams, or similar. Word documents (e-documents).

- **External functionality:** use cases (focusing around mainstream scenarios).

- **Domain model:** class diagrams – first-cut, middle-out from key business entities.

- **Complex business rules:** OCL (not diagrammatic) or a domain-specific knowledge-based tool.

- **Life cycles:** state diagrams for entities (focusing around relevant mainstream scenarios).

- **Internal interactions:** either sequence or collaboration diagrams (for your information).

- **Technical/architecture:** package, component, deployment diagrams (for your information).

These aren't complicated. Like any language, it's hard to start, but once you learn the few basics, you'll begin to understand and communicate your requirements to the IT staff.

Try it. It's easier than you think!

Some Suggested Readings

Allen, Paul, and Stuart Frost. *Component-Based Development for Enterprise Systems: Applying the Select Perspective.* Cambridge University Press, 1998. ISBN 0-521-64999-4.

Bremdal, Bernt, Hjelmervik, Ove R., and Wang, Kesheng. *Introduction to Knowledge Management, Principles and Practice.* Tapir Academic Press, 2001. ISBN 82-519-1660-7.

Fowler, Martin, and Kendall Scott. *UML Distilled: Applying the Standard Object Modeling Language,* 2nd Edition. Addison-Wesley, 1999. ISBN 0-201-65783-X.

Heineman, George T., and William T. Councill. *Component-Based Software Engineering: Putting the Pieces Together.* Addison-Wesley, 2001. ISBN 0-201-70485-4.

Jaaski, Ari (ed). *Tried & True Object Development: Practical Approaches with UML.* Cambridge University Press, 1999. ISBN 0-521-64530-1.

Jacobson, Ivar, et al. *The Object Advantage: Business Process Reengineering with Object Technology.* Addison-Wesley, 1995. ISBN 0-201-42289-1.

McGibbon, Barry. *Managing Your Move to Object Technology: Guidelines and Strategies for a Smooth Transition.* SIGS Books, 1995. ISBN 0-132420-09-0.

Penker, Mangus, and Hans-Eric Eriksson. *Business Modeling with UML: Business Patterns at Work.* John Wiley & Sons, 2000. ISBN 0-471-29551-5.

Svejby, Karl Erik. *Managing Know-how.* Out of print.

Taylor, David A. *Business Engineering with Object Technology: A Manager's Guide.* John Wiley & Sons, 1995. ISBN 0-471-04521-7.

. . . plus many more.

You can also visit our profound business case at *www.Wet-Liquids.com* (however, your hardware of today is most probably not compatible yet for beverage downloads of the future).

Index

abstract actors, 31
activity diagrams, 15–23
  abstract actors in, 31
  diamonds in, 20–21
  process-flow view in, 26
  swim lanes in, 18
  waits, 22
actors, 29, 35, 46
  generic, 31
agencies, 3
aggregations, 52, 54–55
animators (tools), 68
Aonix, 11n, 68n
Apollo 13 syndrome, 39
application frameworks, 77
asset paradox, 4–5
associations, 52–54

automation
  business, 21–22
  examples of, 36–39
  tradeoffs in, 36

Bach, J.S., 9
batch processing, 29
Bergman, Ingmar, 9n
boring life cycles, 64
Bräne, Tomas, 10
building components, 81
business modeling, 13, 27
business objects, 77
Business Process Reengineering (BPR), 4
business semantics-driven strategies, 50

business service-driven strategies, 50
business use cases, 23–25
    e-views in, 26
    standard use cases distinguished
        from, 36
buying components, 80–81

Campbell, Don, 9n
cardinality (multiplicity), 53
certification of components, 83–84
class diagrams, 48–52
    data modeling compared with, 89
class-discovery strategies, 50
classes
    mapping relationships among,
        91–95
    objects distinguished from, 52
    relationships among, 52–53
    state diagrams of, 61–63
class hierarchies, 59
class modeling, 27
collaboration diagrams, 67, 70
Common Warehouse Metamodel
    (CWM), 90n
communications
    among components, 76–79
    in sharing responsibilities, 7
component diagrams, 71
component-driven approaches, 10
components, 76
    bidding process for, 87–88
    building, 81
    buying, 80–81
    certification of, 83–84
    communications among, 76–79
    development strategy for, 73–74
    impact of, 79–81
    libraries of, 83–84
    responsibilities of, 78–79
    reusing, 81–83
    sharing, 84–85
    traps in, 85–87
    used in music, 9

compositions, 52, 55–58
configurable components, 82
configuration management tools, 86
copyright law, 86
customizable components, 82

database schemas, 91
data modeling, 25, 89–90
    diagrams and standards for, 90–91
    mapping relationships in, 91–95
demand-side control, 75
deployment diagrams, 71
diamonds, in activity diagrams,
    20–21
Dijkstra, Edsger W., 69n
documentation, 8
domain analysis, 83
domain models, 99
domains, 32n, 48

Enterprise Java Beans, 85n
entity relationship (ER) diagrams, 90
error handling
    in activity diagrams, 19
    in state diagrams, 66
Erwin (tool), 90
e-views, 26

factories, 2–3
Forman, Milos, 9n

generalizations
    in advanced modeling, 57–58
    in class diagrams, 49–50
    among classes, 52–53, 58–59

human-computer interaction (HCI),
    27–28

IBM (International Business Machines
    Corp.), 10n, 85
IBS (firm), 10, 82, 85
intelligent configurators, 86

interaction modeling, 27
interfaces
    for components, 82
    user interfaces, 28
isomorphism, 48–49

Jackson, Michael A., 61n, 64n
Jacobson, Ivar, 23, 27, 29

Kain, Brad, 97n
key business entities, 61–62
knowledge
    as asset, 4–5
    sharing, 5–6
knowledge enterprises, 3–5
knowledge industries, 1–2
    know-how in, 3–5
    types of, 2–3
knowledge tools, 51
knowledge views, 26
Kratochvíl, Jiří, 9n

legal issues in components, 86–87
libraries of components, 83–84
life cycles, 50, 61, 99
    boring, 64
    state diagrams of, 61–62
    unstructured, 64–66

management-by-exception style, 17, 19
mapping relationships, in data models,
    91–95
methodologies, 8, 36, 48
Mozart, W.A., 9
multiplicity (cardinality), 53
music, 9

Object-Animator, 68n
Object Constraint Language (OCL),
    51, 90
object interaction modeling, 27
Object Management Group (OMG), 4,
    72n, 86

on data modeling and database
    creation, 90
Software Process Engineering stan-
    dard by, 11
objects distinguished from classes, 52
offices, 2
on-the-fly identification, 83

packages, 76
    components and, 82
parameterized use cases, 43–44
pluggable components, 81–82
process-flow view, 26
project management, 28, 33–34
prototypes, 28, 32

Rational Unified Process (RUP), 8–10
responsibilities, of components, 78–79
reusing components, 81–83

Select Business Solutions, 11n
Select Component Factory, 11
Select Perspective, 11, 36
sequence diagrams, 62, 67–70, 72
SF, see WebSphere Business Compo-
    nents
sharing components, 84–85
smart response trap, 42
software
    bidding process for, 87–88
    know-how in production of, 4
    legal issues involving, 86–87
    see also components
Software Process Engineering (SPE)
    standard, 11
SQL (structured query language), 53n
standard use cases, 36
state diagrams, 61–66, 71–72
state-machines, 62n
states, 63
stereotypes, 44n, 90
Sundgren, Bo, 61n
Sveiby, Karl-Erik, 2

swim lanes (in activity diagrams), 18
synchronization bars, 16
system boundaries, 46
system documentation, 8
system use cases (standard use cases),
    36

traditional waterfall project trap, 45
tying-it-here trap, 39–40

UML (Unified Modeling Language)
    methodologies used with, 8
    Object Constraint Language of, 51
    other diagrams in, 70–71
    smorgasbord, 14–15
    standardization of, 5, 8
unstructured life cycles, 64–66
use-case analysis, 36–39
use cases, 27–29

business, 23–25
    example of, 29–34
    generalization of, 33
    parameterized, 43–44
    prioritization of, 32–34
    standard versus business, 36
    template for, 34–35
    traps in, 39–45
use-class trap, 42–44
useless user trap, 44–45
user interfaces, 28

value-is-self-evident trap, 41

WebSphere Business Components (SF;
    IBM), 10, 85

XML Metadata Interchange (XMI), 86n